BE STILL, AMERICA . . . I AM GOD

Be Still, America . . . I Am God

From Out of the Rubble, Stories of Hope

"Be still, and know that I am God;
I will be exalted among the nations,
I will be exalted in the earth."
• Psalm 46:10 •

Amy Bartlett

CHRISTIAN PUBLICATIONS, INC.
CAMP HILL, PENNSYLVANIA

CHRISTIAN PUBLICATIONS, INC.

3825 Hartzdale Drive, Camp Hill, PA 17011
www.christianpublications.com

Faithful, biblical publishing since 1883

ISBN: 0-87509-967-X
© 2002 by Amy Bartlett
All rights reserved
Printed in the United States of America

02 03 04 05 06   6 5 4 3 2

Dedication

Every word, always, is dedicated
to the Lord who authors my life.

This book is dedicated to Diane and Charles Bartlett,
who raised me up in the way of the Lord. Their hearts
and lives were the place I first met Jesus.

And to all those whose lives were lost through
the effects of September 11, 2001 and the families they
leave behind. They are our most recent, noble veterans.
They are the most unexpected ones.

And finally . . . to Mrs. Moore.

September 11, 2001

May this be recalled as the day that America
turned its eyes back to You, the living God.

—Franklin Graham
Family Memorial Service, October 28, 2001

Contents

Part 5
I Love New York

Part 6
There Will Be Mercy Yet

Special Thanks to:

Stephanie Samoy, for endless listening and a helping spirit; Nanci DeSmet for prayer, phone calls, e-mails, 'tips' and exceptional effort; Eric Hogue, who asked me to keep a "journal from the streets of New York" that kept multiplying; Marlene Bagnull, for forwarding the single e-mail that became this book; the Goings, for their prayers, their dog, good cooking and their living room, porch and kitchen table where some of the last portions of this book were written; Doug Wicks and David Fessenden at Christian Publications for proceeding with endurance, wisdom and kindness under such sensitive circumstances; Diane Bartlett, for, at the very least, several titles, incomparable creative influence and guidance as I follow in her literary footsteps. And to Dr. Stace Gaddy for being a greater friend than I could design, especially through the demanding rigors of this assignment; for spiritual direction and encouragement, for being a constant creative springboard and director, and for being the unnamed "friend" in several scenes throughout this book.

And for graciously taking precious time to share personal stories during difficult days:

Tim Mercaldo and Paul Schooling from Gateway Cathedral in Staten Island; Frank Silecchia, Father Brian Jordan, Steve Lee; Dona and Herb Fisher for telling their story and the Dobson's, and Kathi Wilson for fielding communication; Stanley Praimnath and Dan Van Veen; the gentlemen of Ladder Company 25 on Manhattan's Upper West Side; Peter Hannaford, William Faye, Holly and Jeff (last names withheld); Joyce Hart, Dave Odgers, Billy Boyd, David and Sandy Epstein, Sam Jimenez, Sr., Ed Morgan, Father Michael Duffy, Steven Connolly, Mark Reamer, Lisa Beamer, Doug MacMillan (for patient and diligent correspondence), Joe Smaha, Brian L. Overby, Max Lucado and Karen Hill.

Introduction

We were not ready. We weren't expecting it. But God was ready and moving, knowing.

We all have our senses—women's intuition, maternal instinct, business sense, gut feelings. Mothers have had dreams of children in danger and awakened just in time to save them. Loved ones have fallen to their knees in prayer the moment their loved one is in peril thousands of miles away.

I think somewhere in the back of our minds we suspected that if something this world-changing were going to happen, we would feel it coming. But we were all taken quite out of a comfortable sleep.

It couldn't have been a more common morning, run-of-the-mill in responsibilities, but the weather—the sky—went beyond common and well into perfect. The *New York Times* called the day's conditions "Severe Clear."

I listen to 1010 WINS news radio in the morning. They note the exact time every couple of minutes. I usually leave at 8:45, but I was running just a few minutes behind. By my calculations, I must have locked my door the moment American Airlines Flight 11 hit the North Tower of the World Trade Center. Locking my apartment door—a simple task, like the tasks everyone had at that precise flash of time. Little did I know I was locking the door on innocence in the United States. The next time I stood at my own front door, I would live in another world.

I wouldn't know the news for a while. During my commute, I was completely out of the loop. Walking to the subway, waiting for a train (they kept running without announcement on the north end of town until nearly 9 a.m.)—so close, yet I knew nothing. I was com-

1

pletely unaware that within walking distance, both landscape and
lives were being traumatically and permanently altered—unaware
that men were sitting in first class on other planes waiting for their
chance to conduct horrible mayhem. How does one not sense it?

But this once, we were withheld from advance knowledge; we
were allowed to learn a terrible lesson. So I kept walking, unknowing.
The world kept turning, about to know.

There were no extra crowds on the subway. There was no ominous
sensation. We rushed and clamored like any other day. People
talked loudly, put on makeup, read newspapers—stories that in minutes would mean nothing at all. I was reading a book, oddly enough,
about a wartime photographer and the unusual elements of life in a
time and place of war. It seemed so distant, both in time and place.

The train ran smoothly to 34th Street. I stepped out of the subway
doors and that's the first snapshot memory I have of that day: the or-
ange posts with the black signs that mark 34th Street (the last stop
for this train), the dirty tile walls and the yellow lines for standing behind when a train is approaching. There was an announcement.

"All service has been suspended for all trains south of Canal Street."

I was sure it was a mistake, the transit announcer's first day on the
job. Shut down all lines for all stops below Canal Street? I may have
even said it out loud: "Something really big must be going on." Perhaps
someone tried to rob the Federal Reserves.

I was still expecting a normal day but finally picked up a strange
feeling, mixed unconsciously with jealousy for an hour ago, when
the world's great new wound hadn't yet been opened. But no one
was murmuring yet. No one knew.

I could have picked up other clues. The spiritual world was displaying signs of unrest to unusual degrees. Coming up out of the subway
just steps from Herald Square, I saw a Yellow Cab bump the Livery cab
in front of it. A fender bender at this chaotic corner is not uncommon,
but this one immediately escalated to frightening intensity. It was one
of those confrontations where you slow down and look around you,
looking for cover just in case. The Livery driver roared so fiercely, I expected a gun. The Yellow Cab driver looked terrified but shouted back,

opening his door, one foot out. A third man came into the street from the sidewalk—a short man with wide shoulders, silver hair and a look of wisdom.

"You," he said with a fierce but fatherly force, "get into the car." And then to the other, "You, get into the car. You go . . . you go." He smacked both cars and when the Livery driver protested, the third man raised his force another notch. "Go! You go now!"

All three had individually distinct accents, but rang somehow as distant brothers. I don't know what would have happened had the third man not been there. It was a small replica of the world stage here on the corner of 34th Street. It would soon become our duty as America to be the third man coming in from the sidewalk with "fierce but fatherly force" to construct peace between distant brothers. Only this time, it was us whom they had hurt most, on our own land, on such a beautiful day.

By the other end of the block there were more pieces to the puzzle. There were officers in sharp blues at every entrance of the Empire State Building—decorated officers, not beat cops. The streets were filling up with people who were supposed to be at work, who were upset. Something was off.

A Hasidic man said to the officer standing in the revolving door at the westernmost entrance, "You don't understand. I have to be in my office—it's very important today."

"No, you don't understand," the officer said with "extra" information behind his voice, "no one . . . is going into this building."

I knew something major was in progress but I didn't think it would be something the world would know about. I thought I had been coincidentally exposed to privileged information along my route—the announcement in the subway, the comments of a lone officer on 34th Street. I thought I had a story for my colleagues when I finally got to work. *The* story I would find them watching was an unfathomable thing.

At the corner of Fifth Avenue, if I had looked up, I would have seen two tiny towers smoking in the distance. I didn't take the time to look up—getting to work was still a priority, and being on time.

Within the next couple of hours, almost everyone on the island would be sent home from their jobs. Priorities change fast.

I got on the elevator with another woman who works for *Guideposts*. She heard the first piece of news from the doorman. I had seen her ask him. A plane had hit Tower One of the World Trade Center. We said little in the elevator; it was nothing but a surprising story, probably one that would fade. After all, in 1945 a B-25 bomber had hit the Empire State Building. The towers are so much bigger; surely there was minimal damage.

In the reception area of the twenty-first floor, I was standing in the doorframe of the entrance when I heard about the second plane. Without a doubt, that would change the world. I thought that in coming in late, I would be breaking the news to the book department upstairs. But there was already a society gathered in the conference room.

The crowd itself was heartbreaking—these were quintessential New Yorkers. Most of them New York natives, magazine editors, veterans of the local scene, people who greatly love this city. To this day I haven't fully processed how the room felt.

The images played without pause on the television in the corner. A few people went out onto the roof to see if they could see from where we were. Because of the layout of the taller buildings attached to the back of ours, we could only see the cloud of smoke heading out toward Brooklyn.

It was a dual image. On the television screen before the window, you watched the cloud, the distinct shape, the momentum, the color. Divert your eyes a few inches, and there it was in the sky, through the window, acting as if it were real. But it just couldn't be.

One of the women in the office had a brother who worked in the towers. He was a perpetual early bird, Stephanie explained. And if his tendencies matched hers, it was likely he was early—she'd been known to be more than a half-hour early in the morning. As the drama unfolded, she stayed in her office calling anyone who might be able to find her brother. It was the only thing to do at the time. We all checked in on her from time to time, bringing her updates and encouragement, but feeling helpless to help or understand.

Again, I was in the doorframe—it seems I spent the whole morning under a doorframe, perhaps an unconscious attempt to seek protection—when the first tower fell. It was obviously inconceivable, especially to this local crowd, who had spent more time in, near or around the towers than most of the viewing world. A wave of theories flashed through the room. As fast as a brain works is as fast as we assumed everything but the truth.

We thought, *The terrorists had planted bombs on each floor and what we saw was a series of bombs going off—but the tower is still there.*

We thought, *Something fell from the top and there may be great destruction—but the building is still there.*

We thought, *Anything, but surely the building is still there?* Then the column of smoke began to clear . . . and the building was not there.

I had to tell Stephanie it had come down. I knew she still hadn't found her brother. Of all the images I'd watched in a million clips that morning, I hadn't fully grasped any of them until I watched her absorb what had happened. I didn't believe my own words; I didn't know how she was going to believe me. But her face made everything clear. It became my vision of the human reaction to the reality of the loss.

Her brother, she would later find out, was just fine. He was one of the many who found themselves running unusually late to work. He never even made it off the train—commuters had been returned to the first stop in New Jersey. He and hundreds of others who had been headed to their own jobs in the towers stood safe across the river and watched the steel towers crumble—their livelihoods, their friends, the substantial buildings in which they'd placed their lives every day: the black marble floors, the complex network of elevators and security checks, the stunning view from their offices. They stood in the park and watched it all go—safe and far removed.

I had to take a few minutes away to call my parents, who had each left tremulous messages on all my phones—and I needed a break from processing the news. My mother's call came not only from a frantically concerned mother's heart, but also from a radio producer's. From a studio in Northern California, my mother kept me either on the air or close by the phone for the greater part of the morning. My office is on the opposite side of the building from the conference room and I couldn't stand being isolated from the news or from people for too long. There was a need to be informed and not alone. But this kept me running back and forth. Literally running.

I noticed a few hours into the ordeal that I'd put on a new outfit that day. I suddenly wanted to take it off. This was not a day for new clothes.

I had on a sleeveless shirt and sandals. It was a warm and perfect day. It was the lingering end of summer mixed with a crystal clear sky, the kind of sky that seems always to have birds playing against its backdrop.

I kept all the phones poised to call the radio station at a moment's notice. On some incidents I was able to reach them before the news agencies could. When the progress of the attacks kept pouring in, I wondered if I would still be in the office at nightfall. I didn't expect it to stop where it did. I was unsure about leaving.

The Pentagon had been hit. . . . There were unexplained fires in DC. . . . There were planes unaccounted for still in the air. The President was informed of the events while he was reading a story to a group of elementary school children in Florida. He nodded his head and then, for the sake of the children, this man—our President, who was only beginning to prove his estimable spiritual mettle—continued reading to the children until he finished the book. Only then did he leave calmly to do whatever he humanly could to run the world with the other men and women he'd prayerfully chosen at his side, trusting even in the midst of such chaos that God was on His throne.

Shortly after the plane came down in Pennsylvania, it was decided we should all go home. The Empire State Building, directly west of us, was an intimidating presence. Personally, I wanted to remain safe on the top floor of our nearby building. With what I'd just seen on television of my own city—not of a far and foreign land—I did not want to release myself into the street where there was no concrete umbrella under which to hide. But I couldn't stay.

There are only ten of us in our department on the split-level 22nd floor, three of which lived outside of Manhattan and therefore couldn't get home just yet. All bridges and tunnels were closed. They went home with the editor-in-chief, who lives only a few blocks

away. I called them later when I'd arrived home; tł ∞
sandwiches. Life goes on.

But there was a long path between those hours—
ing on the street corner together as a group and split
all our individual homes. I said good-bye to the peopl
and I stood still. *Where am I, Lord? Is this still Manhattan?* I was trying to gauge how much my world had changed. Was it a singular in-
cident, or would this day continue to progress until we looked like a
sci-fi movie with Lady Liberty sunk in Hudson Bay? Extreme, sure,
but only hours before, the towers reduced to fourteen stories of rubble had also seemed an extreme exaggeration. Now it was the view.

I hadn't noticed that it was the view until the middle of my wondering daydream on 34th and Madison. The downtown end of the
avenue focused itself in my vision and I saw the smoke. It seemed a
different color than on the television screen, or in the air where I'd
watched it from the roof. Here, it was a new hue. It was the color of a
cotton ball run through ashes.

I was still on that corner, back on my cell phone with my mother and
getting ready to go back on the air with her and Eric Hogue to walk the
listeners through the scene, when two cars came screaming through
the intersection on a collision course. The light was red for 34th Street
when a black, unmarked vehicle, its siren blaring, didn't give enough
warning to the cross traffic on Madison, and barreled into the side of a
tiny old Ford.

From the middle of the intersection, two well-dressed women got
out and ran absentmindedly to the nearest corner, which was mine.
The driver stayed with the car and pulled it to the side away from
danger. One of the two women was sitting on the sidewalk holding
her knee in passing pain. Neither was visibly injured, only jostled. I
knew of nothing I could do to help but to lay my hand on their shoulders and say, "You're OK." One of the women looked at my hand as
if the feeble offer of comfort was so unexplained that I wondered if
she had heard yet of the devastation down the street.

Someone asked if anyone had a cell phone to call 911. Mine was
up to my ear. I admit I had a selfish moment of not offering my own,

but it was because I knew these women didn't need one and weren't going to use it even if offered. Additionally, I was waiting to go on the air and it had taken me nearly twenty minutes to find a channel for my call to go through. Fortunately (otherwise, I would have felt terrible), I had assessed the situation correctly; a cell phone appeared from the crowd and the women turned it down.

There was another woman beside me, just as unsure about what to do next and just as overwhelmed. She shook her head at me in mutual sympathy and hugged me. I remember her shocking pink lipstick and a ponytail on the side of her head. The world had become a place where this unlikely stranger and I would hug without exchanging a single word, while sirens screamed by. It wasn't even lunchtime yet. She patted my shoulder once more before she left, and I was on the air.

Asked to look around and recount what I could immediately see, I noticed the last detail of this accident: The drivers of both cars were exchanging license and registration information. Wherever the driver of the unmarked car had been headed, with lights and sirens blaring, it was delayed long enough to write down the name of their insurance carrier. Again, life goes on.

I stayed on the corner for almost an hour, realizing progressively that my common surroundings, what I passed each day at lunch, were now the outer epicenter of the world stage. I described over the phone what I didn't think would be of interest, but in hearing reaction from the other side of the continent, came to realize fully where I was standing and what I was seeing. It was History—the colors of the ambulances that blared by, the street sign that said, "City of New York." Even when turning my face into the crevice of a building to drown out the noise and keep the cell phone signal strong, I found the images reflected in the windows of the building. I could not escape History.

I signed off for a while to make room on the air for official reports and began making my way home. I had only forty blocks to go, which was nothing compared to the hours and miles that most would be walking home that day. I also remembered those that would not be walking home at all. I was so grateful for my forty very small blocks.

Unbelievably, I found a cab after about ten blocks. I had been headed up Fifth Avenue to my church, but with the surprise of the empty cab, I suddenly wanted to go home. "75th Street, please, between Columbus and Amsterdam."

"I'll try," the driver said. That was a new one.

We cut across town at about 45th Street. The crowd shots I'd watched all morning were now first person through my cab window: random groups of very vulnerable-looking people watching building-sized news screens in Times Square, watching for what to do, wondering how to feel. Shocked is such an unworthy word for the shape of their shoulders.

Through the lines on the cab's back windows I took several pictures of the gray columns on the Times Square monitors with the stock market ticker in red and blue running across the bottom. Something about the view from a taxi's back window, pulling away, made me feel like I was leaving a best friend behind. Along with the rest of the Tri-State area, I would feel like that for a while, between missing people and missing buildings. It left a gaping hole in both the seen and unseen. The old world was gone—another friend to add to the list of casualties.

We got across town and almost up to Lincoln Center before the cab driver told me to get out. He didn't even want to try anymore. Just sitting in traffic that far had already run the meter to $13 for only half the way home, almost double what the whole trip would have cost on a normal day.

Alongside the busy intersection of 66th Street, a mom-and-pop electronics repair shop had parked its van out front with all the doors and windows opened, turned the radio on full volume and left it there, keys in the ignition, for people to get the news. Television was out for those who didn't have cable, and radio would be all we had for a while. For their community, they trusted the keys in the ignition on a busy New York City street.

A variety of neighbors and passersby hung on all corners of the van, listening and adding whatever other news we'd each picked up in our own travels. People moved on as they became satisfied or saturated with information, but others would quickly fill their empty spot.

Home was only a few more blocks for me. But something about the calmness, safety and relief was actually more unsettling than anything I'd seen or passed so far. While my mother and her on-air partner kept me informed of West Coast information (such as the fact that the malls in Sacramento had closed), here in New York, it was eerily life as usual. The restaurants were full—somewhat silent, but full. Starbucks was open. I can't help but repeat that the weather couldn't have been more perfect. It was a blue, blue day.

I was home by 3 p.m., with no idea what to do next. My house was not in ruins. There was no damage to clean up, no bandages to tie. Nothing was wrong with the immediate picture—not even a room-mate to verify that the day had even happened. I was largely lost in a sense of "what now?"

Calling the church to say I wouldn't be coming, I realized why it was that I'd opted to go home instead: I wanted to prove to myself I *could* go home. So many of my friends and acquaintances were unable to get off the island, having lost the contest for the last spot on a single available ferry. Others were wounded or missing. Going home was a test: to see if I could get there, to make sure it was still there at all.

Manhattan is a unique place to be caught in a crisis of this magni-tude. You can't swim across the river. The tunnels and bridges, if for-tunately not collapsed, are at the very least closed. You are at the mercy of emergency measures. If a road is closed, there is no detour. You can't cross a field to get to an access road. You can't get out without government-administered arrangements. But that's part of what makes New Yorkers cling to one another. We're stuck together here; we'd better be ready to work together. We'd better be a step closer to realizing our own legitimate brother and sisterhood.

There is definitely a noticeably missing spirit in our community from what has been lost. But it was replaced immediately by a new spirit that had been missing before. In the "what now" we would find a more genuine loyalty, a kindness and responsibility. We would fi-nally be good to one another.

I got up my five flights and put the key in the lock. It halted me. Everyone had taken a voyage that day. Only some would come back home to unlock their door. But everyone's world was new. Everyone's home had been struck. I walked into my apartment and sat down on the floor beneath the window where the sun was coming in. Later, I would go back on the air for most of the afternoon. More vans would park in the street below and blast news radio. I would even go back downtown that night. But for a while, for a long while, I stayed perfectly still at the foot of my windows, with the old green frames and pots of plants, with the perfect sky and a shining silver radiator. I did nothing more than sit, and feel the sun.

I seriously debated sharing the "day of" details from my humble vantage point. *What was my story,* I reasoned, *considering instead what others had gone through?* Somehow it seemed the very telling of it was disrespectful to those whose lives had truly been shattered into new pieces that day.

Primarily I agreed to because I was asked, and encouraged that it was important for the sake of those who had not been here at all. But as I began writing, I discovered what mattered.

We all have a story. They are intricately individual and unique. But behind them and within them there is one story weaving the strongest thread. There is God.

Whether we knew Him, or acknowledged Him, or not, He was there in complete love. He knew us before we were "knit . . . together in [our] mother's womb" (Psalm 139:13). He knows the number of hairs on our head (Matthew 10:30). He knows where we were and what we felt those first defining moments on the 11th of September—fears, needs, hopes, loss.

And He provides. No matter who, what, why, where or when, in every story there is the light of the Lord casting His eyes to our heart to stay, "Be still. I am here; know that."

It was in this coexistence of difference and sameness that I saw life—normal life.

On any given day any one of us is dealing with circumstances that are vastly unparalleled, yet so much the same even in their difference. One parent is holding his child's hand and watching him battle a ravaging disease while another parent's largest concern is his little one's first day of school. One family is safe in one another's loving arms their whole life long, while another is torn apart by death or divorce or dissension.

Our stories are always just as different as they were on the 11th—when some were at home making breakfast for their toddler while others were on the 91st floor of Tower One. But they are also always just as "same." There are the same needs and fears, the same answer calling for our attention. There is the same hope available to all. We are, more than we know, blood relatives. All of us.

So we tell all of the stories, every single different and same one, to show entirely the one story in them all. To show the big picture where a familiar God becomes recognizable within such different lives.

I also have to acknowledge what is *not* in this book. Though the people and stories that build its pages are phenomenal, I appreciate the enormity of what is still left to be told.

Between the tens of thousands directly involved with the World Trade Center, the hundreds at the Pentagon, the families of travelers and the fact that there is no one in the world whose life was not somehow impacted, it is impossible to tell the whole story. Even on a smaller scale, we are nowhere near being able to include them all because of time and freshness of pain.

I share only what it is time to share, and the rest will unfold in its own time.

But the stories here will take you from Colorado to Atlanta, from Sacramento to Philadelphia, from Fort Drum to (of course) Ground Zero—stories with widely different circumstances but the same Source of strength and direction. You'll find first-person accounts of those headed into the direct path of danger who were spared by phone calls, car failure, broken alarm clocks, canceled trips, missing keys and—ultimately—the hand of God. Other stories can only be told by the loved ones left behind. But even through their great loss, enduring the unimaginable, they tell their stories with resolve, hope and even gratitude for the Lord who sees them through.

I am not insensitive or ignorant to a nation and a world of different people who depend on different comforts and beliefs to see them through. On the contrary, I am responsively sensitive and therefore wish them the greatest comfort that exists—the most eternal one. Further, I wish God the fulfillment of His heart to see everyone He loves safe in His hands. This is why I tell my story, and theirs, and His all together—that your heart and God's may be full, that you may see His hope and grasp it.

I don't expect the world to become stable. I don't expect the right decisions always to be made or peace always to prevail. I know there is evil in this world and that we're slow on the uptake to turn completely to God, so evil seeps through by choice. But I do know how I can make it. I do know hope. He proves Himself daily. It is because of Him—by Him, through Him—that we can find the calm assurance to face whatever tomorrow may bring. An old song says it best: "I can face uncertain days, because He lives." We, as a nation, a world and a family, can face anything, because He lives.

Part 1

A New City on the Hill

*You are the light of the world. A city on a hill cannot be
hidden.* (Matthew 5:14)

I remember what Lower Manhattan used to be. Upscale green mar-
kets, enclosed sunlit crosswalks twenty feet above the street and
wide-open plazas. Hotels, global financial institutions, the United
States Reserves. I met friends there for lunch and ate pretty much on
the water. I sat in folding chairs while gifted quartets filled the gal-
lery with reverent song. There were palm trees inside that stretched
toward the glass ceiling that might as well have been the sky. And
that was just the ground floor.

Imagine 108 flights up at Windows on the World on a perfect day.
Or further, to the observation deck where you stand on top of the
crossroads of the world and the wind is so fierce you feel it must be
the force of the earth spinning. Here, so far above the ground, you
imagine you can feel the centrifugal force. You are holding on, flying
forward.

The tip of Manhattan will never be that same world again. Now in
unbearable ugliness, it is more excellent than it has ever been. It will
break your heart even standing blocks away from the furthest rim of

15

the wreckage. But men and women keep pouring in to help. They won't go home.

What has happened here, in this place unlike any other, is oddly enchanting. What people have become to one another, what ordinary human beings are willing to do, what physical, emotional and spiritual pressures they are willing to endure, are all telling a story that hasn't been told quite like this ever before. There has been war. But this is a strange new war. Our civilians have become soldiers, chaplains and heroes all. They can't even estimate how long it will take to clear the wreckage, much less consider what will be done with the land and the memory. But they are already building a new city on the mound of debris, a city of brotherly love, of sacrifice and tenacity, of sweat and tears that keep falling. They are building a city of hope, and with their own hands making an active show of faith. They need no pulpit. Meet them, watch them. They give their life as their message.

This is an amazing new city on the hill. These are people I want my children to know. This is the world I want to live in. I am proud to tears. As our President said, standing amidst the rubble, "The whole world can hear you." They can see you too.

Let your light shine.

A Roadway in
the Wilderness

The West Side Highway—also known as the Henry Hudson—is a great drive. The majestic Hudson River to the east changes outfits every day: some days dim and dreary; glitzy black and gold on a warm city afternoon; ice blue in the perfect days of autumn. That stretch of road has always been destined to be more than just traffic, construction and a place where even the nicest of us didn't exactly get along all the time. Now, it's come into that time.

On the West Side Highway there has appeared an amazing new village inhabited by an all new breed of family—though not really new, as this is the type of family we've always been meant to be to one another. But it's our current fortune since September 11 that it is indeed happening. I say "fortune," not at all disrespectful of the pain endured as the cost of this change. But it could have gone the other way—dissension, exacerbated hatred, crime and judgment. And that would have had a terrible effect on one's sense of hope, to think, *If such an event wasn't able to heal us and set us right with one another, what unimaginable horror would it take?* I believe—I hope—that it will take no more than this that we are experiencing.

"God Is in This"

One of the best evidences of this is the thriving community that has set itself up on the lower West Side Highway—beginning, oddly enough, at Church Street.

There are respite centers set up in tents where rescue workers are instructed to rest for thirty to forty-five minutes. They'd like to take

17

ten or fifteen-minute breaks only, I'm told, but their commanders won't allow it. A person doing such work, seeing such things, needs to rest.

In these respite centers, clergy have come from all over the tri-state area to minister, but also just to "be there"—ministers, pastors, priests, rabbis. One pastor I interviewed, Paul Schooling from Gateway Cathedral in Staten Island, had a heart that was crystal clear over the phone as he told me the stories of people he'd come to care about and the "congregation" that the people of Ground Zero had become.

"If you come and drop off tracts on a table," Paul began, "you really don't get the picture. You have no idea what was really going on, who these people are individually, what they're going through, and what they want to talk about.

"You have to spend time here . . . days. You have to be here whenever they need you and even when they don't need you. They have to know you're there. You have to spend time here like it's your family—just like building a relationship with anyone. Just like building a relationship with God."

He says he and the others have tried to do just that, spending as much time there as possible to connect on a truer level with the workers.

"When they walk into the respite center you can see them slow down." With that image you could hear him start to remember, and then he began to tell the stories that have unfolded during the days at Ground Zero.

Traveling through the Manhattan-bound side of the Holland Tunnel at about 5 o'clock in the morning, Pastor Schooling was stopped by two police officers. There was no one else around. He assumed he was about to be asked for his credentials. Noticing Paul was clergy, one of the officers said he'd like to ask him some questions about a book he'd been reading. Paul geared himself for a tough question, a tough conversation. Was it a book about the end times—Armageddon? No—it was The Prayer of Jabez, the best-seller based on a biblical character's request to God for blessing, prosperity and protection (see 1 Chronicles 4:10).

The author of the book, Bruce Wilkinson, says that part of Jabez's prayer, to "enlarge my territory," is a request for God to increase one's circle of influence. The officer said he was struggling with being able to pray like that, feeling like it was selfish or focused on personal gain.

Paul said, "Let me ask you a question now. When you took your oath as an officer, didn't you do it to put others above yourself, to put yourself in a position of service and ability to serve?"

"I knew it," the officer replied, "I knew I had it all wrong. God wants to use me in a bigger way right where I am." *That* is prosperity.

And I could see the scene: 5 a.m., in the middle of an empty roadway. Talk about being used "wherever you are"! God had planned at this time and place to teach this man whom He loved a new truth—one that his heart had been longing to learn. And there was excitement in his voice now, and a different climate in the tunnel.

Pastor Paul, who acknowledges he's barely a small part of this, since it's God who changes lives, hadn't yet reached his destination that morning, where one would assume the ministry was going to begin. He was in the tunnel, on the way. He reminded me during our conversation that we all need to be ready and willing, even "in the tunnel" when it's 5 a.m. and you are focused on a destination and a purpose that is somewhere else, sometime later. God can use you anywhere, anytime. The pastor and the cop were both learning from the same God—and from one another—a little more about being ready and willing to hear and heed His voice, wherever you happen to be.

There was more healing for the hand of God—more comforting and mending what had been broken. And He wasn't only focused on what had broken within the 9-11 events. He was watching every pain and hearing every hope and coming even to heal the homes of those giving their lives to help others.

One man approached Paul and said, "My life is a mess—can you help me? I'm out here removing the rubble and I've realized what a mess I've made of my marriage." He talked about his relationship with his wife and what he had taken for granted. He had even filed for divorce. I don't know how many days it took, how many conversations, but somehow he got back to the pastor and shared the news that he and his wife are getting back together, and there was great joy in finding what nearly had been lost.

Barely able to keep up with his own words, Paul remembered two officers—Housing Police—who had apparently been partners for a while, and began to tell their story. It was one of serving together and loving one another, partners on the police force, and the kind of bond of trust and commitment that is created there. It was about sharing your heart and your faith. And it was about a moment in time which Christ had known since before time began.

"I know God's in this," one of them began, "but how could He allow it?" It was about 4 o'clock in the afternoon, and among the great new "tribe" of people inhabiting the tented village on the West Side Highway, the conversation began that just about everyone is having right now. How could God allow any of it—good and evil in the world? They're tough conversations to have at a time like this. They come with some tough answers.

The same officer continued. "I'm tired." He just put it out there. "Not physically. I'm tired of running away from God."

The pastor offered, "You know, you can hand that over anytime. He knows that there's no way we can handle it on our own. You're not expected to be able to."

Smiling, he replied that these were all the same things his partner had been telling him all along, but he didn't want to listen.

"Do you pray?"

"Yeah, it's the same thing my buddy, here, tells me. He says, 'Pray.' I do pray. I pray to get through my day all right, to get home safely. I pray for things other people need around me."

By now a smile had crept up from his partner and he smiles back.

"I know why he's smiling, though. He'd say I haven't prayed the biggest prayer. I haven't prayed to invite Him to come in and stay."

"You can do that now."

"Now?"

I wish I could have been there to watch this man as he considered this. I wish I could have known what his face looked like, if he had family, how many seconds passed before he said, "OK, but is it alright if I pray with my partner?"

"Well, you certainly don't need me."

He asked his sergeant if he could take a couple minutes.

"Sure, but the Reverend has to stand guard with me."

There they were, the sergeant and the Reverend, standing guard, partners in duty and in service, while an officer prayed with his partner, his long-time buddy, who had told him so much about a Lord who loves them both. Now together, they came to Jesus, in uniform and on duty. There was exceeding joy and celebration in heaven, so the Bible tells us. But for starters, it's enough for me to imagine this scene, under a tent on an empty highway alongside the Hudson River.

There were others too, as Paul spent more and more time just being friend and brother to those who had become "the locals" of this new community. There was the coroner who would come to give him a hug and say, "I'm all right, but keep praying for me." There were the two brothers who worked for the asbestos decontamination area. Each time they came through they'd say it was probably the last, that they'd be moving on—but they kept coming back. People would ask the pastor, when he'd been gone for a couple of days, "Where have you been? I really need to talk to you."

Another conversation reminded me that it's not just the clergy that bring the light of the Lord to the table. For all of us, it's our job, our privilege, to have the guts to tell of the glory.

There were three police officers talking about the inspiration of the scene, how people have come together. "It's so good." Three very simple, but poignant words. "It's so good."

"Can you imagine?" one of the officers said. "Usually these people would be bickering, fighting, territorial, departmental. I mean, they've come from all over the place." He cast a good-humored glance at the Reverend when he added, "I know you'd probably say God is in this."

But a female officer beat him to it.

"He doesn't have to say it, I'll say it: God is in this."

Well, there goes the separation of church and . . . anything else at all.

In my own life, I'm remembering to look around and realize, "God is in this." When you see it, say it too. For there's no situation in which it's not true. Sometimes it takes a while to figure it out; sometimes you have to trust that He really does use for good what was intended for evil; sometimes you don't see the full story for years . . . or ever. But no matter what the subject or the surroundings, you can look around and say, "I don't have to hear the Reverend say it, I'll say it: God is in this."

A Cross in the Valley

So other than the tents for rest and respite, camaraderie and food, what else would a new community need? A place to work and a place to worship. They've found both to a powerful degree at Ground Zero.

One of the most common phrases about the site is an exclamation of its size. It's always whispered when you get to that phrase for emphasis. "The size of it . . ." "I never imagined . . ." "You have no idea . . ." "It's just so big."

But in the middle of one particular canyon, in a scooped-out, new-millennium translation of the valley of the shadow of death—made of nothing but twisted steel and crumbled concrete—the construction workers noticed something. Almost exactly in the center of the valley, standing on its end and perfect in proportion, was a cross.

They began to notice other crosses too, not quite as exact but close, lying sideways with longer or shorter shapes. Some still stuck up high on the gutted stories jutting above ground, some lying flush across the rubble. But this particular one had planted itself upright in the bowl of the valley. The reaction of the workers to the cross and the place around it was passionate, but I wonder if they could have known to what degree history was beginning.

"Gentle giant" and "angel in a hardhat" is what the newspapers and networks are calling him. He's Frank Silecchia, an ironworker with Local 731, and he's the one who first brought the story of the cross to life, jump-starting what will become an amazing voice of history.

I met him in front of Lincoln Center in his huge old black Ford Bronco, the perfect vehicle to characterize this man who has spent his

23

days in twelve-hour shifts at Ground Zero, driving back to Jersey every night. It was already a museum, this truck. He had pictures and news articles tucked everywhere, along with medallions and gifts he had been given from an astounding collection of people. There were poems from children, a beanie-bear from the Oklahoma bombing memorial (with "The Survivor Tree" emblazoned on its beanie chest) and, of course, a photo of his son Noah.

As we looked through some of his photos from the site, the story came in remembered pieces. I heard it painted clearly in the sound of his voice when he said, "It's unbelievable tyranny down there."

He had been working in the area of that valley and had just helped remove three bodies from the rubble when he looked up and saw "Calvary."

"I've seen this picture of Calvary with three, four crosses in it. The main structure of Christ's cross was in front of me. It took my breath away."

I find it poignant that he had just removed three bodies when the sight of redemption struck him.

He came to others and said "Have you seen this?" They had, and had been moved as well, but Frank began to put the cross to work for the purpose for which it was intended. It indeed became a place to visit Calvary.

"What does the cross mean to me?" Frank reflected. "Healing, joy, faith, salvation—not only from sin, but from all that we're facing, especially down there in that pit." People had already begun to be renewed. There were three EMS workers, one dealing with so much she'd almost become nonfunctional. She said she felt renewed after coming to see the crosses. It became a place to sit, meditate, cry, think, pray—a place just to stop for a while and rest at the foot of the cross, both spiritually and literally.

You didn't need to name the place—it had already named itself with the random gatherings of people who came to focus on God. But just so there was no question, and so others who hadn't been down there yet could know, Frank took a spray paint can and painted the words

"God's House" on all the surrounding wall fragments . . . with arrows for direction. He led them to the cross.

With the shadows and glints of all the broken windows, and the enduring faith of a people unbroken, it became the most beautiful cathedral in the world. This place was holding to hope and faith literally on top of the results of evil and devastation. They were putting God into it—inviting Him, for a change. And the reunion was a powerful one. In the comfort of the shadow of that cross you could hear Him say, "I never left you. . . . I've been here all along."

A parade of visitors came through to find the same message standing there. And Frank took them all down to the valley to visit "God's House." He took Jeb Bush down, and Benjamin Netanyahu. He shook his head at that one. "I took the former Prime Minister of Israel to Calvary!" He found it beautiful. He added, "Solid man, strong handshake."

There was a visitor from the Vatican who left him an angel medallion to keep. As we talked, Frank lifted his identification pouch hanging from his neck. The medallion was tucked in the bottom of the pouch.

Then there was Barbara Walters. She had come with her niece and her niece's husband. They had lost their son and were looking for a little closure. Talking to Frank she asked, "How could you tell me God's here?" Boy, had she asked the right man!

"Can I take you to God's House?" He took her by the arm to help steady her across the debris, serving as her anchor on the way. She said, "I need a picture of that . . ."

One retired rescue worker had come by, whose son had been buried. Frank assured him, in the shadow of the cross, that all would be well. "Thank you," his new brother said. "You've told me words I will write down for when I am in despair."

The loss of a son and the need for words to heal in times of despair brought to mind another powerful note. Of the many small publications that came out around town immediately after the tragedy, designed to provide such "words to heal," there was one called *Remembrance: Fallen but not Forgotten*, from the King's College at the

Empire State Building, in partnership with Priority Associates
(www.iPriority.com). At the end of the opening page was this short
paragraph:

> Hatred cannot win against a society that stands tall
> when kneeling on bended knee. Hatred cannot win
> against hope. Like the dust around us, so much is still
> unsettled. For a while, the questions shouted from our
> souls may drown out the whispered answers that time
> and wisdom wait to tell. Yet, though our souls ache,
> there is hope. In our darkest hour, there is hope: carry-
> ing us, counting every tear, knowing us and aching to be
> known. For in all that mankind has ever chosen to wor-
> ship, the God of the Bible stands alone as the only God
> who ever lost His own child.

There was another visitor whom Frank knew he'd been looking for
all along. Father Brian Jordan, a priest at St. Francis of Assisi parish
in Midtown, was offering communion to workers at the site. Frank
took him, too, to see the cross and the wheels started turning again.
The prayer of Frank's heart was that the world could have this cross.
"I want everybody to have it just as Christ wanted everyone to have
salvation."

In the following letter from Father Jordan, we hear his portion of
the story in his own words:

The Healing Cross of Ground Zero

> On Tuesday, September 11, Tower One of the World
> Trade Center collapsed on top of a smaller structure,
> World Trade Center Building 6. The collapse went
> through the roof and completely gutted its interior. Nu-
> merous lives were lost and the destruction of property was
> astronomical. On Thursday, September 13, Frank
> Silecchia, a construction worker, was searching through
> the debris for possible survivors. All he found were dead
> bodies and arranged for them to be exhumed for a proper
> burial. While in the remaining structure of WTC 6,

Frank came upon a sight that truly moved him and greatly awakened his Christian faith. In front of him, he saw a perfectly symmetrical, cross-like structure in the midst of the debris on the ground floor of WTC 6. Frank believed that, despite the tragic and catastrophic attack against the World Trade Center, the presence of God was evident through that cross. Frank also noticed that there were about five other steel, cross-like structures in the same rubble but none as perfectly symmetrical as the first cross that he found. He then painted the words "God's House" along the walls of the remaining structures of Tower One and WTC 6.

Frank showed the cross to many rescue workers, firefighters, police officers and other construction personnel. They were also humbled and moved by the sight of the cross. Frank talked to engineers who believed that the cross most likely came from Tower One when it collapsed on top of WTC 6 and landed in that position. Frank has appointed himself as the guide to "God's House" and showed many people this sign of faith. Among these people were visiting clergy members who were also inspired by the sign of the cross. Frank felt compelled to have the cross excavated and preserved as a visible sign of God's presence at Ground Zero. During the time period of September 13-23, he experienced difficulty in carrying out what he thought was his mission from God—preserve the cross!

On Sunday, September 23, Frank encountered Father Brian Jordan who was distributing Holy Communion among the rescue workers at Ground Zero. Frank showed Father Brian "God's House" and the Franciscan priest had a deeply moving religious experience. The cross represents the pain and suffering of the crucified Jesus Christ. It also represents the redemption of the risen Jesus and redemption for all humanity.

So strong was his experience that Father Brian con-
tacted the First Deputy Mayor Joseph Lhota of Mayor
Giuliani's administration. Deputy Mayor Lhota heard of
this cross and directed Father Brian to contact the
Mayor's Commissioner of Art and Design, Ken Holden,
for the excavation and preservation of the cross. Commissioner Holden received permission from Mayor Giuliani
to undertake this project. Commissioner Holden then directed the Ironworkers Local 40, who had a contract with
the AMEC Construction Company, to remove the cross
from WTC 6 and place it on top of a concrete median on
West Street, between Vesey and Liberty Streets.

*[Author's Note: Frank gratefully acknowledged Danny Collins, Fore-
man for Breeze Demolition, for his character and efforts, along with
the others, in retrieving the cross from its resting place in the rubble,
and its transfer to the place it now stands.]*

This took place on Wednesday, October 3. On
Thursday, October 4, there was a blessing ceremony at
the site of the healing cross of Ground Zero. October 4
is the feast of St. Francis of Assisi, who is the patron
saint of ecology and is known as the mirror of Christ.

The blessing ceremony included testimonies of faith
from a firefighter, a police officer, a Port Authority officer, an iron worker, a construction company official and
the founder of the cross, Frank Silecchia. Father Brain
Jordan blessed the cross through the Rite of the Christian Blessings but pointed out that this is a symbol of
faith for all people and it is now America's Healing
Cross at Ground Zero. About 400 people attended the
ceremony and it was well covered by the press. Since St.
Francis is also the patron saint of animals, Father Brian
blessed two police search dogs—Atlas and Keifer. He
also blessed a group of volunteer veterinarians from the
Midwest and then proceeded to bless all the partici-
pants and the ground on which the cross stood. This is

now America's cross and may the healing begin for our great nation.

On behalf of all the uniformed personnel and construction workers at Ground Zero, we respectfully request that the Healing Cross at Ground Zero be a part of a permanent memorial of the World Trade Center disaster. Future generations need to be reminded that we New Yorkers saw evil at its worst and goodness at its best. Goodness was revealed in how New Yorkers came together and fellow Americans poured in endless support. In turn, the community at Ground Zero wants America's Cross to be permanently preserved. Why? The cross symbolizes Jesus Christ as both Victim and Victor. Christ was, from a human point of view, a victim of senseless violence. He was betrayed, denied and abandoned by his apostles except for one. Christ was a victim of unfair trial and scourging along the way to Calvary. However, Christ was Victor—He was victorious over death through the resurrection. America, like Christ, is also victim and victor. America was victimized by the senseless terrorist attacks and many died. America is also the victor by pulling together as a united country and rebuilding once again. America's Cross represents our present suffering and our eventual victory over terrorism.

—Father Brian Jordan, OFM

Author's Note: Father Jordan is a Franciscan priest who lost twelve good friends at the World Trade Center disaster. He has been ministering among the men and women at the site since that day.

"Announce the Cross"

"It's my job now," Frank said, finishing his story, "to announce the cross."

He described the first time he was actually able to grip the steel beams that make up the ten-ton, eighteen-foot cross. "I felt the power of the cross. Not just *this* cross, but *the* cross. The image of the cross is sometimes tarnished; sometimes despair turns us away from it. But here we were able to turn *to* it in the midst of despair, and it healed."

"I felt like I could lift this thing," Frank said of the structure that towered over him. "Jesus carried my cross, it's the least I could do to carry His out of the rubble and give it to the world."

We'd been talking for almost two hours, and though he was genuine and sincere from the start, this is where his heart truly became evident.

"You can't control man's destiny through evil. Man's destiny is already written and it's written in salvation and victory. It's up to us if we want to be a part of that.

"God does not desert us in our hour of need. Evil has a way of claiming some people—but only from this life. There is eternal life that is in God's hands alone. And in His hands, no one can harm you. Terrorism is the devil's tool; the cross is our tool. And I don't think—I know we'll win.

"The people that went in to those buildings are not only America's heroes, they're God's heroes. They gave their life without question and they did it to save others.

"I think this should be called the valley of heroes—topped by the symbol of the greatest hero, Jesus, who gave His life not just to save some, but to save all people. He was in the building too, meeting the same need He met on the cross 2,000 years ago."

If it is a valley of heroes, then Frank Silecchia is one of them. He wouldn't accept that title—just as most of the men down there would not. "I'm just a soldier in His army," he says. Both as a Christian man and an ironworker, he's "just doing his job."

But something was born here that I believe will be a uniquely powerful part of history. If all the channels are cleared to make this cross a part of the permanent memorial at Ground Zero, then for centuries at the least, thousands will come to try to understand what happened that day, and as they do, they will look to the cross.

It is the only place there are true and lasting answers, answers with the power save—not just in a day of tragedy, but eternally. There is no greater comfort that could be poured into that site and the human hearts around it. There is no greater name to heal and restore. There is no greater love.

At some point in the evening, Frank handed me a rumpled old flyer from the Billy Graham prayer center here in NYC. On the front there was a picture of this cross as it was originally found in the center of the valley of rubble. Across the face of the photo are these words from Steve Lee, Executive Director of Peace Officer Ministries and the chaplain to both the Colorado Springs Police Department and the U.S. Bureau of Alcohol, Tobacco and Firearms. The whole cross-at-ground-zero experience, in just a few inspired words:

From God's house
Fired new from dying flame,
This living sign remains,
Arms outstretched, embracing yet,
Our avalanche of pain,
To still, to fill, to heal again.

Amen.

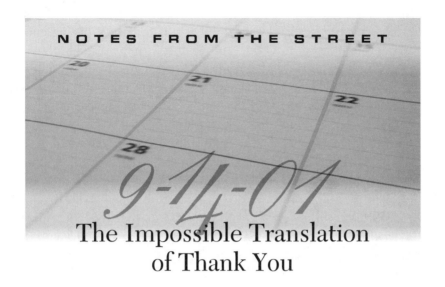

The Impossible Translation of Thank You

Included throughout this book are five articles written from the streets of New York in the days following the air strikes. The series was inspired by this first message, which was originally written not as a chapter, or even as an article, but as a letter. Its style reflects that fact—it is informal, more personal, less polished. But it was the beginning of everything, including this book, as you'll find in the conclusion of the following, the inspiration for Be Still, America.

It's such a disorienting time—the days are so heavy and yet I'm surrounded by people who have lived through incredible trauma or are looking for their loved ones—that I feel like I certainly can't complain. Everyone, it seems, is carrying conflicting emotions: gratefulness for one's own safety, life and health; sorrow over the burden of individuals, but also of the whole nation; the tension of possible events to come. No one quite knows what to feel.

You begin to feel a bit lighter; the President prays, the navy sings "Glory, Glory Hallelujah," you're back to work with nonessential tasks; you begin to "shake off [the] dust" (Isaiah 52:2). But then you pass by a sign of someone's husband, child, brother or fiancé who's missing, and you want nothing but to sit down in the dust with them and hurt.

But I am fine . . . wonderful, really. I was evacuated from my building at work. I walked most of the way home. I saw none of the direct destruction, and only a few of the indirect results: a car accident due to mild hysteria; smoke and ash; burning smells, even up by my home on 75th Street, when the wind shifted Wednesday night.

Amy McConnell, a dear friend of mine, worked in Tower 2 on the 51st floor. She was in the lobby when the windows blew, saw the second plane hit from a drugstore down the street and ran—in heels—up to the 59th Street Bridge, then all the way back down to the south tip of Brooklyn. The Brooklyn Bridge didn't reopen until evening. She walked from 9 a.m. to 2:30 in the afternoon. But she's alive and well, which is what counts.

The number of people that "happened" to be suddenly sick that day are astounding. The news media can say whatever they want, but the personal stories suggest that there were more headaches, backaches, sore throats, sniffly noses, medical appointments and business trips than imaginable. Of the 70,000 people who could have been in the Twin Towers on that day (50,000 regular residents and an estimated 20,000 visitors, tourists, delivery, etc.), only an estimated 5,000 are currently on the missing persons list. I know 5,000 is a vast number of individual lives, but when considering how many either got out safely or were "somewhere else" that day, well, the stories are going to start pouring out.

Nowadays, the trains are running—but minimally, so you're not sure at all which one is going to come into your station or where it might be going. But you get on and hope it lets you off within walking distance of your destination. (It's really not bad; they're running close to normal, but there's a sporadic change here and there.)

Television was out completely for a couple of days, at least for those who don't have cable. (The transmitter was the red and white tower on the top of the North Tower [WTC 1] and the only one in Manhattan.) They weren't acknowledging this on any of the stations, whether TV (via cable) or radio—which also meant they'd said nothing about when we could expect transmission to be restored.

This was more disconcerting than one might think, because it's not about television. It was that, to be alone in a room where every channel is not even snow, but black, is a constant reminder that something's wrong and it's so bad that the "grown-ups" can't fix it yet.

Then a friend called Thursday night to tell me they'd made an announcement that ABC was broadcasting through sister UHF channels (25, for me) and that CNN had somehow patched into network channel 11 (WB). I thought it was extraordinarily kind and understanding that they sent CNN even to the cable-less few.

Later that night the local CBS affiliate was restored to its rightful channel. I know this sounds trivial, but what a difference it made in restoring a sense of normalcy. One tiny piece, but it was enough to get you through to the next level of rebuilding.

I ventured down to the West Side Highway yesterday to see if I could help. They're saying they have an abundance of volunteers, which is somewhat true, but my personal opinion is that they're telling us "civilians" to stay home because for every hard worker there were five or six just creating more chaos. We were trying to hand out water, Gatorade, etc., to the trucks of men and women coming in and out of the site. Many didn't stop as food and water were everywhere—even beyond the barriers where "official" groups had taken trucks of food/water into the actual site. But the ones who hadn't gotten supplies elsewhere would roll down their window and ask for whatever they wanted.

This was a fine plan until people started mobbing the cars and throwing food through the windows. Police had to be stationed on the corner to periodically tell the "helpful" folks to back off. I could see the looks of frustration on the faces of the workers, especially the military personnel, all of whom had spent their day seeing unthinkable sights. I know I couldn't possibly understand.

There were the truly helpful as well. Strangers cried on each other's shoulders; a woman and two men who were hanging up missing posters also took the time to pass out masks to those who needed them. No one was arguing, not even in the subway, where it's usually a given that someone's going to shout a few choice words.

Among the greater lessons of this tragedy, people have learned to practice simple courtesy. The best sentiment I've seen on a sign all week was not on the front of it, but on the back. On the West Side Highway, people have gathered for quite a distance to wave signs and cheer and express their gratitude for the workers—military, police, search and rescue, fire, medical—who are at Ground Zero, enduring the sights and sounds there. The signs read things like, "New York collapses, New Yorkers rise up," or, "We are all today the USA."

But on the *back* of one was written in marker, "Dear New Yorker, this sign is yours, use it enthusiastically and leave it for the next New Yorker." Of course, I had to take a picture of that one.

I have to tell you that the hardest thing yet, other than the disturbing images on the TV or in the papers, was to see, late the very first night when I went out to get a cup of coffee, a fire truck that came rumbling slowly up 46th Street. It was covered in dust and worse: on every outjutting lip of the truck, concrete chunks had gathered. They were large pieces, so close up that I could see the black specks that you see in concrete. (Of course, they won't let civilians near the site, and since I wasn't there when it happened, this was my first real-life image.) I thought, "There goes the World Trade Center—the towering, immovable structure of stability—broken to pieces and being dragged about the city so far from where it's supposed to be spending the night."

Actually, much harder than that is trying to lie down and go to sleep, knowing I'm within walking distance of people who are trapped, scared, alive and breathing. I'm too close. I'd rather be closer—at the site, digging with my own bare hands—or further away, removed completely from the task of "getting on with New York."

When I began this letter, I intended a few lines, a paragraph, maybe, just to let you know I was all right and to thank you for your priceless thoughts and prayers. But I suppose I needed someone to talk to, after all. Everyone here knows all of this already and to an extent, we want to

talk about something else for a while. But once a day you have to un-
load the events of the day and leave it all in the Lord's hands.

Speaking of which, here's the best one I've heard yet, from Mary Ann
O'Rourke, executive editor for *Guideposts* magazine. Her friend passed
on a sentiment that had been passed on to her. I'm not sure where it
originated, but it continues to multiply as I've told many others myself.
"Put your hand on your pulse," she said. "Do you feel it? Now repeat to
its rhythm: 'Be-still . . . and-know . . . that-I . . . am-God.' "

Now if we can just do that not only for ourselves individually, but
also as a nation: reach for our pulse, our life-blood, the One who
gives life, and "know" this. Hear it to the rhythm of His heartbeat,
together as one. "Be still, America. Be still and know that I am God."

May His peace of mind be with you in any way you find yourself in
need. And if you get a moment, ask Him where you might be needed in
the midst of all of this. Tell your family how much you love them. And
thank God for this opportunity to fully realize the blessings of life and
freedom.

Grace and comfort to all of you.

Part 2

Pray without Ceasing

Rejoice evermore. Pray without ceasing. In every thing give thanks: for this is the will of God in Christ Jesus concerning you. (1 Thessalonians 5:16-18, KJV)

We must pray literally without ceasing—without ceasing; in every occurrence and employment of our lives. I mean that prayer of the heart which is independent of place or situation, or which is, rather, a habit of lifting up the heart to God, as in a constant communication with Him.

—Elizabeth Ann Seton

Conversation, strength of relationship, cultivation of love, understanding God and one another. These are the endowments of prayer. And that's barely the beginning.

Prayer is not a stale, outdated thing. It has not been made obsolete by technology and intellect. It's not obligatory or ceremonial. Its limits are not two aching knees bent at a bedside in the evening.

Sometimes prayer is being angry with God, struggling to understand, asking the tough questions. Prayer is never unheard.

the loudest speech. It reaches to the One who holds the
﹍﹍ᴄ, who moves the clouds and calms the seas, only to illumi-
nate the fact that He is as near as can be. Prayer ushers you into the
Oval Office and sets you beside the president. Prayer places you at
the shoulder of the enemy.

Prayer can move the tangible on the other side of the world, or
take what seems intangible—emotions, fear, depression—and dis-
mantle it. Prayer changes what seems to be fact.

Prayer is personal and individual, yet the voice who answers it is
the same. His character is constant and familiar. As we become more
intimately acquainted with Him, we can recognize Him in a
stranger. He is the same Father, who meets us individually.

People search endlessly for power nowadays. There is no greater
power on earth than prayer, and yet prayer is the understanding that
we are not in control at all.

Prayer is not a formula for success. It's not a checklist or a magic
spell. Prayer—most of all—is faith. It is faith and trust in God who
has encouraged us, "Do not be anxious about anything, but in everything, by prayer and petition, with thanksgiving, present your re-
quests to God. And the peace of God, which transcends all
understanding, will guard your hearts and your minds in Christ Jesus" (Philippians 4:6-7).

ｉ The Five-Fingered Prayer ｊ

When it's hard to know where to begin with prayer,
or to remember what to pray for, I start with my hand.

I hold my hand in front of me and begin with my
thumb pointing toward me. The thumb reminds me to
pray for those closest to me—my family, my friends, my
neighbors. Though it may sound silly, teachers point in
school, so as I come to the pointer finger, I pray for
those who have been my teachers, mentors and spiritual leaders. The middle finger is the largest one. This

brings to mind, and to prayer, the leaders of our country; our government, our military, our President. The next finger is called the weak finger. With it, I remember the weak, the sick, those who are poor and hurting and in need of help. Saved for last are my own needs. I leave them for the little finger, but I lift them to the Lord, and know His eye is even on the sparrow.

When my hand is closed, I find it holding the Savior's hand.

—Anonymous

The National
Importance of Prayer

A Story from James and Shirley Dobson
and Herb and Dona Fisher

*"Just one example of what God
does to bring us to pray together."*

Herb Fisher just meant to go fishing. Just a common fishing trip. He couldn't have known that God was beginning to move the pieces that would play a part in the quilt of events that brought our nation together in prayer.

Herb Fisher and his wife, Dona, live in eastern Pennsylvania where, among so much else, Dona is the National Day of Prayer Coordinator in her county. Under normal circumstances, this would have nothing to do with her husband's plans for Tuesday the 11th. But as we all know, Tuesday that early September was not normal circumstances.

Herb decided to take a two-day trip to Jackson Hole, Wyoming. By morning, he found himself suddenly stranded far from home. He was among many that morning making phone calls and alternate plans, trying to figure out how to get home to family in a time of crisis.

In talking to the local airport officials, he was encouraged to drive to a larger international airport that would most likely be opened before the smaller one in Jackson Hole. So he hit the open road as so many others did that morning—a somber, national, great-American road trip—and drove nine hours to Denver, Colorado, only to find that airport closed as well.

The next possibility was Atlantic Aviation, a smaller terminal used by private jets. Herb has a private jet, but he never likes to use it for just one person—it's not economical. But he decided the circumstances warranted it; he felt the need to hurry home. He put in a call for one of their pilots to come through Denver to pick him up as soon as they were given the go-ahead to reenter the now-empty American skies.

While waiting, he befriended a man in a similar situation—both of them sitting and waiting around, trying to get home. This man was also headed east, specifically to Washington DC. And as it turned out, he just happened to be a partner of Signature Airways, the place where they were waiting. Seeing this as an opportunity to put another passenger on the jet, Herb invited him to ride back with him.

It was a greater provision than either of them knew at the time, because for the rest of the day, only private jets with a part 135-charter license were permitted to fly. The gentlemen probably wouldn't have gotten home that day. Fortunately, the jet for which Herb had called was one of them—actually the fourth in the United States to fly the skies that day. It was on its way to Denver to pick the two men up.

One hour before the airplane arrived, Herb received a call on his cell phone. It was Dr. James Dobson, president and founder of Focus on the Family, located in Colorado Springs. To Herb, he's a friend.

"Herb," he began, "I don't usually ask favors from you, but President Bush just called and invited Shirley and me to attend the National Day of Prayer service."

It was a personal request, and a serious one, as Shirley Dobson is the chairwoman of the National Day of Prayer. Representatives of our country's praying people were gathering in the nation's capital. Attendance played a poignant role in support and morale.

"Herb, can you get your jet here to pick us up?"

"Jim, guess where I am?"

"Where?"

"Jim, I'm at the Denver airport. The jet will be here in about an hour."

"I can't believe it!" Jim responded. "Can we ride back with you?"

Herb said, "Of course," and hung up to call his wife.

"Pack your bags!" he said to her. "We're going to Washington, DC for the Friday service!"

In a couple of hours, the airplane was on its way with four passengers. But it still wasn't over. There were yet more details God had arranged to cover.

Access to Dulles Airport in Washington DC was closed. Without the proper credentials, you couldn't land. But to the surprise of the others flying that day, the stranger that Herb had befriended in the Denver airport had the proper connections to clear arrival at Dulles. Without them, none of them would have been able to land in Washington DC—the location of the National Cathedral and the National Prayer Service, their final destination.

All of it was God, gathering unto Himself a congregation of people ready to pray for this nation. It was orchestrated, every piece. The service was not only a memorable experience. It was a public and collective opportunity to come before the Lord, to bear witness to the peace of mind He delivers, to ask Him to sustain His mercy on our country, to love and be loved by One who directs our steps.

About the details of how this story unfolded, Dona Fisher writes, "How good it is to know that 'the steps of a good man are directed by the Lord' " (Proverbs 20:24, paraphrase).

By the Light
of the Eastern Shore

On Friday after the attacks, America was planning a rolling candlelight vigil at 7:30 p.m. in each time zone. I called and e-mailed everyone I knew, and then I forgot. I took the subway home and turned the corner from Central Park West onto 75th Street, and there it was. One lone candle sitting by itself. No person in its attendance. Just a candle in a little glass cup. It wasn't even dark yet and its light matched the shade of dusk. Dim, fiery.

I actually ran. I felt as if I had let someone down. Big, New York commuter bag bobbing off my shoulder, business suit and tennis shoes, I ran down my street and wondered if anyone else was doing this crazy thing. It was only just now 7:30 and as I ran toward Columbus, they started to appear. Tiny groups of people that you never, ever see just standing around in the evenings. I mean this is New York, and the Upper West Side at that. We don't meet in groups on the sidewalk at dusk. These were my neighbors by a block. I'd always known they were up there somewhere in their apartments, but only by faith, not by sight. I'd never waved to them before, but I did now.

I ran the rest of the way home and up five flights of stairs. I told my neighbors on the sidewalk, "I'm coming right back down." I grabbed two homemade candles someone had given me, jumped into a pair of jeans and ran back downstairs. In that short period of time, someone had come by and written a Nelson Mandela quote in several bright colors of chalk, something about becoming a better community or a better mankind. His dog started to eat the chalk and he moved on to another street. My landlords looked at the quote and said things had gotten way out of hand. That broke the ice, as the rest of us found it funny, and after two years in this building, I introduced myself to my neighbors for the very first time. "Hello, my name is Amy; I live on the fifth floor . . ."

I had my phone in my back pocket and a friend called. He had just walked out of our church, Calvary Baptist on 57th Street, and was on his way over to join us, but he described the scene across the street where a crowd had gathered outside of Carnegie Hall to sing hymns. It didn't look like they were a professional group—just people. But they were the typical lot from midtown New York: vibrant, talented, determined and passionate. "I love this city," he said. "Listen to them; it's the sound of one voice, singing harmony."

It was 8 o'clock. In half an hour, the Midwest would pick up this vigil. But for now, the light was shining from the Eastern shore. And it wasn't just the candles; it was the heart, the hymns, the hope. It was my new neighbors who had been there all along. And about three miles away, it was the circle of prayer that surrounded a smoldering Ground Zero we couldn't get our minds off of for a moment. This is the New City on the hill, and the tip of the island has become hollowed, hallowed ground.

Covered by the Word of God

I know there are 50,000 to 60,000 personal stories—at the least—from the people who were in the towers on the 11th, or nearby in schools, offices, churches. I acknowledge that this is only one story. The singularity is in his front-row seat. It narrows the field of similar experiences the minute Stanley tells the part of the story where he "turned and saw United Air Lines Flight 175 heading straight for him."

He ducked under his desk, not much of a match for a jetliner at full speed, but he leaped underneath. On top of the desk was his Bible. He was unbelievably, sheltered.

But I'll let him tell you his story.

Surviving the 81st Floor
of World Trade Tower Two

A testimony of God's hand
of protection amidst tragedy

As told to Dan Van Veen

Tuesday, September 11, 2001, began like any other day for Bethel Assembly of God deacon and Sunday school superintendent Stanley Praimnath of Elmont, Long Island. He got up early, took a shower, prayed, got ready and headed for work.

The drive was uneventful. The train ride was the same. Yet this day, he would see the hand of God spare his life. "For some particular reason, I gave the Lord a little extra of myself that morning [dur-

49

ing prayer]," Stanley said. "I said, 'Lord, cover me and all my loved ones under Your precious blood.' And even though I said that and believed it, I said it over and over and over."

When Stanley arrived at World Trade Center Tower Two, he took the elevator up to his office on the 81st floor. "I work for the Fuji Bank Limited," he said. "I'm an assistant vice president in the loans operations department. The company is located on the 79th through 82nd floors."

Stanley greeted Delise, a woman who had arrived before him. After talking briefly, he headed over to his desk and picked up his phone to retrieve his messages. "As I'm standing there retrieving my messages, I'm looking out at the next building, One World Trade, and I saw fire falling through from the roof," Stanley said. "Now, this entire building is surrounded by glass, and you can stand up and from there you can see all the buildings, planes and everything flying at the same altitude."

As Stanley saw "fireballs" coming down, his first reaction was to think of his boss who works in that building. He decided to try to call him to see if he was OK. "I'm dialing his number, and getting no response. So I say to Delise, the temp, 'Go, go, go—let's get out.' " Delise and Stanley got on the elevator and went down to the 78th floor. Some other people were there. The company's president, the CEO, the human resources director and two other men joined the group and headed down to the concourse level of Two World Trade Center.

If they had continued on and exited the building, all of their lives would have been spared. As it was, that's not the way it happened. "As soon as we reached the concourse level, the security guard stopped us and said, 'Where are you going?' Stanley explained about seeing the fire in Tower One. According to Stanley, the guard said, "Oh, that was just an accident. Two World Trade is secured. Go back to your office." That turned out to be fatal advice—aside from Stanley, Delise was the only one of that group to survive.

"We were joking, and I told [human resources director] Brian Thompson, 'This is a good time to think of relocating—it's not safe anymore.' " Stanley headed back to his office, but before he got there, he told Delise, that with the events of the day, she should go home and relax.

Thompson went to the 82nd floor, the president and CEO went to the 79th floor and Stanley got out on the 81st floor. When Stanley got to his office, his phone was ringing. "It was someone from Chicago calling to find out if I'm watching the news," he said. He told the caller everything "was fine." But everything wasn't fine—far from it. As Stanley was talking, he looked up and saw United Air Lines Flight 175 heading straight for him.

"All I can see is this big gray plane, with red letters on the wing and on the tail, bearing down on me," said Stanley. "But this thing is happening in slow motion. The plane appeared to be like 100 yards away." I said, "Lord, You take control, I can't help myself here." Stanley then dove under his desk. "My Testament [Bible] was on top of my desk," explained Stanley. "I knew, beyond a shadow of a doubt, that the Lord was going to take care of me, once I got there." As he curled into a fetal position under his desk, the plane tore into the side of the building and exploded. Miraculously, Stanley was unhurt.

However, he could see a flaming wing of the plane in the doorway of his department. He knew he needed to get out of his office and the building fast. But he was trapped under debris up to his shoulders. "Lord, You take control, this is Your problem now," he recalled praying. "I don't know where I got this power from. But, the Good Lord, He gave me so much power and strength in my body that I was able to shake everything off. I felt like I was the strongest man alive." All the while, Stanley was asking the Lord to spare his life.

"I'm crying and I'm praying, 'Lord, I have things to do. I want to see my family, Lord, help me through.' "

Stanley's office resembled a battle zone—walls flattened into dusty heaps, office equipment strewn violently, flames flickering about and rubble everywhere. "Everything I'm trying to climb on [to get out] is collapsing and I'm going down," he said. "I'm getting cuts and bruises, but I'm saying, 'Lord, I have to go home to my loved ones. I have to make it. You have to help me.' "

Suddenly, Stanley saw the light of a flashlight. For a moment, it stunned him. *What were the chances of someone bringing a flashlight to this floor?* he thought. "My first gut reaction was, 'This is my guardian angel—my Lord sent somebody to save me!'" Stanley began screaming, "I see the light, I see the light."

But after clawing his way through the debris, he realized that he couldn't get out—all the exits were blocked and his "guardian angel" couldn't get to him—a wall was between him and the staircase. "He can't get to me and I can't get to him, and by this time I can't breathe," Stanley said. "I don't know if it was sulfur or what [burning jet fuel, perhaps], but I can smell this thing. I got down on my knees and said, 'Lord, You've got to help me. You've brought me this far, help me to get to the staircase.'"

But then Stanley did something surprising. While praying on his knees, he called out to the man behind the wall, "There's one thing I got to know. Do you know Jesus?" The man replied he went to church every Sunday. Then they prayed together, to enable them to break through the wall.

"I got up, and I felt as if a power came over me," said Stanley. "I felt goose bumps all over my body and I'm trembling, and I said to the wall, 'You're going to be no match for me and my Lord.'" Moments later, he punched his way through the wall and, with the help of the man on the other side, was able to squirm his way through the hole.

"The guy held me and embraced me and he gave me a kiss and he said, 'From today, you're my brother for life.'" But the danger wasn't over. The man on the other side of the wall, who introduced himself as Brian, was an older man and they still had 81 floors to walk down, with the building on fire and, unknown to them, in danger of collapse.

"We hobbled our way down, and at every floor we stopped to see if anybody was there, but nobody was, except a man who was on the floor, and his back was gone, and he was covered in blood." Stanley asked to be allowed to carry the man out. But a security guard told him it would be better to send somebody up. When they finally made it down to the concourse, only firefighters were there. "They were saying, 'Run! Run! Run!' They were telling us to run out, but they were not concerned about themselves," he said.

Stanley and Brian would have run from the building. But now, the concourse was surrounded with fire. Wetting themselves under the building's sprinkler system, they held hands and ran through the flames to safety at Trinity Church, about two blocks away. "I wanted to go to the church to thank God," Stanley explained, "As soon as I held onto the gate of that church, the building [World Trade Center Tower Two] collapsed." Stanley and Brian made their way safely out of the danger area.

Before they parted, Stanley gave his business card to Brian in hopes of contact at a later time, and said, "If I don't see you, I'll see you in heaven."

Cut and bloodied, with clothes tattered and wearing a borrowed shirt, Stanley finally made it home hours later to his wife, Jennifer, and his two girls, Stephanie, eight, and Caitlin, four. "I held my wife and my two children and we cried," said Stanley. After thanking God for sparing his life, Stanley told God whatever he did, it will always be for His glory.

"I'm so sore, but every waking moment, I say 'Lord, had You not been in control, I would not have made it.' "

"Your Mission, Should You Choose to Accept It . . ."

There are prayers that help us last through the day, or endure the night. There are prayers of friends and strangers that give us strength for the journey. And there are prayers that yield our will to a will greater than our own.

—President George W. Bush, September 14, 2001
National Day of Prayer and Remembrance

It had barely been twenty-four hours since the towers had been hit and I was feeling utterly useless. This was what I've always been prepared for: ministry, help, war.

I'll do anything, I thought, *just to be of service. I have to help.* And like much of the rest of the world, it was driving me crazy. To be so ready and to be told to stay at home.

I tried. I called the hospitals. I watched the news with pen in hand ready to write down an address or instructions. I would have gone to Kmart and bought a hundred blankets and passed them out. I would have cleaned toilets in the Bowery. I would dig with my bare hands if they would let me—and I was not the only one. One young man packed a backpack filled with fliers and a flashlight and made it to New York from California in three days—without a plane—hoping to "get in there" to look for his precious wife.

In later days I would have a few opportunities to help out a little more. But on this very disorienting "day after" I felt like God was telling me to stay home. It wasn't just God, it was the mayor. Repeatedly he pleaded, "Please, we are absolutely inundated with volunteers. We are so saturated we've had to dispatch much-needed police officers to monitor volunteer-heavy areas. And the police have much more important tasks at hand right now."

But the mayor doesn't understand how the Lord works, I argued. *He doesn't understand divine appointments and the need to "be there" when someone turns around and needs to grab a hold of Jesus.* Now mind you, I'm sure the mayor understands this just fine. But I was desperate. I couldn't sit in my tiny little apartment alone and do nothing. I had to walk the corridors of the downtown hospitals. I had to stand with the families of the missing on the sidewalks outside the Armory where they were waiting, hoping and singing, "This Little Light of Mine." Staying home would be "hiding it under a bushel," when I would rather "let it shine, let it shine, let it shine."

Now this is a fine motivation most of the time, to want to serve, to want to get out there, get your hands dirty and help. But I knew deep in my heart that for whatever reason, God didn't want me out there that day. He was telling me no. But I didn't listen—at least, not right away.

Obstinate, I grabbed my keys and the pocket Bible I'd borrowed from a friend and went downstairs to my car. I turned on the radio and sat for a little while, still knowing I shouldn't go but still hoping the mayor would get on the air and say, "I spoke too soon; I take it all back. We need more volunteers. Here's the address—please come out if you can." No such luck.

And I could still hear God like a parent saying, "You know you're not supposed to turn that car on."

I even had a New Yorker moment where I thought, "Well, of course I can't go; I'll lose my parking spot."

After about twenty minutes of this, I turned off the radio and accepted it. But in doing so, I also realized and admitted my main influence was my own selfishness.

"Fine, Lord," I said. "I won't go. But what about me? What am I supposed to do to calm my own heart? I can't go back to that empty apartment and sit there when I know what's happening in this city. And I can't even seem to pray, though I know that would solve a world of what troubles me."

There was no immediate answer, so I locked the car and resigned to moping around the neighborhood. I didn't even know where I was going. I just started to shuffle around the block.

When I came around the corner of 72nd Street, I encountered a woman there, yelling about something—an older, black woman, well-dressed and yelling obscenities about another woman who, by the way, I never did see.

"I may be old," she said, "and maybe I've drunk some in my day, but I'm not out here beggin' and causin' all sorts of trouble. Crazy woman, can't even take care of yourself. What's wrong with you?" (I'm editing for younger audiences, of course!)

She aimed half of these sentiments in my direction as I passed her, and I admit I gave her a slight look that said, "Lady, with everything going on in the world today, how can you give someone so much grief? Lift up, don't tear down." Ironically, I was ignoring my own advice in that one simple action.

And that was it, boy! I'd made eye contact and now she was after me. She changed direction and followed me down the street.

"What was that you were lookin' at me for? Do you have something to say to me?"

Turns out I did. I turned around and met her with my mouth half open and ready to speak. No idea what I was about to say. Probably wasn't going to be my finest Christian moment, probably not what Jesus would have said to her. But that's when the Lord steps in, moves you out of the way and says, "Thank you; *now* I can get My work done."

Now that I wasn't complaining about where I wanted to be or what I wanted to do, now that I had unwittingly followed where He was leading—*now* He would do what He had planned.

ɔn't remember most of what I said to her. I do remember we
.d about accepting that there is evil in the world and remember-
, God's big picture. That there is evil, but none of it is more powerful than He and none of us are out of His sight or beyond His
reach.

> For I am convinced that neither death nor life, neither
> angels nor demons, neither the present nor the future,
> nor any powers, neither height nor depth, nor anything
> else in all creation, will be able to separate us from the
> love of God that is in Christ Jesus our Lord. (Romans
> 8:38-39)

She expressed her sudden fear of people in this world and I had
the chance to wrap my arms around her and call her my family. It
must have been what she was dying to hear because she held on, and
suddenly I cared very much for this woman.

I had an opportunity to say, "We have one Father in heaven and
you and I are sisters. And in the midst of these frightening events,
He's given us that. You and I, in Him, are blood relatives."

He didn't just meet her on the corner of 72nd Street. He met me,
too, and taught both of us while He had our attention. I walked away
having learned three things:

First, I learned that God's work is not always where you think it is.
(This is a lesson I have to learn two or three times a day.) He didn't
need me in Union Square at the prayer vigil. He had the hospital corridors covered: He had the Armory sidewalks covered. He had sent
someone else. What He did not have covered was the corner of 72nd
Street. It would be so much easier if I would listen the first time.

Second, I realized that, with everything happening in this city and
around the globe—and the magnitude of events—He cared about
the tiniest needs (almost insignificant by comparison) of two people
He loved. Yes, He was in the homes of young mothers who had lost
their husbands and had to comfort their children. Yes, He was at the
side of the wounded as they healed and cried for what they had seen.
Yes, He gave His strength to the men who worked without resting to
find their buried brothers.

But He doesn't choose who needs Him more. He watches every sparrow. He knew that this woman, whose name I never even asked, would need His arms today to hold her. He knew where she would be and He met her there.

He even saw my need that day—though I have a hard time calling it a *need*, knowing what others are going through. He saw that I wanted to be used to comfort, to hold, to calm someone who was alone. My arms were empty and He filled them. At the same time, He took us both into His own arms, met our needs in one great gift and sent us home.

And the last thing I learned that day? That it's very important to remember, especially at a time like this, that you are wherever you are for a reason. No matter what your role or station in life, no matter what your city, it is very important to be who you are, where you are.

Acts 17:26 says, "From one man he made every nation of men, that they should inhabit the whole earth; and he determined the times set for them and the *exact places* where they should live" (emphasis added). But it's not just that—it's *why* we are set there that carries the real power and passion. The very next verse explains it: "God did this so that men would seek him and perhaps . . . find Him" (17:27).

Even two people that already knew Him needed to seek Him more that Wednesday, so fresh from Tuesday the 11th, and to get a firm grip of His hand through one another before going any further.

And it's not just about us seeking Him—it's His seeking us. One minister in the midst of the rescue efforts described our unusual circumstances with Jesus' familiar parable about the lost sheep: "Suppose one of you has a hundred sheep and loses one of them. Does he not leave the ninety-nine in the open country and go after the lost sheep until he finds it?" (Luke 15:4).

"What this parable tells us," the minister continued, "is that God cares about the particular, the individual, the last body left in the rubble."

I submit in addition that it isn't just a promise to those literally lost in the rubble, but those lost in any sense. Lost from finding His love, lost in despair, lost in heartbreak. He comes for the lost, no matter

where they are, and as the parable says, He carries them home in His
own two arms to the safest of green pastures:

> And when he finds it, he joyfully puts it on his shoul-
> ders and goes home. Then he calls his friends and
> neighbors together and says, "Rejoice with me; I have
> found my lost sheep." (15:5-6)

He lays us on His shoulders. He rejoices. He rejoices so greatly that
He calls others to share in the joy. And this for no other reason than
that He has found His sheep whom He loves . . . and there's not a single one He doesn't love.

I still bump into a slight sense of helplessness now and then. But remember that even when there are no stories and you feel completely
incapable of helping yourself or others through whatever's around the
corner, remind yourself everyday of the gripping power of prayer.

If a mustard seed of faith can move a mountain, then it can
remove a mountain of rubble. A single prayer is enough to move a
steel beam, and then another. Even instantly, a prayer can lift the
weight of the world off a rescue worker's shoulders, as He lifts the
weight of the world from the ground.

Wherever you pray, that *is* Ground Zero—your car as you run er-
rands, your kitchen sink as you wash dishes, a quiet corner of your
home where you get on your knees. They are all the very center of
Ground Zero.

Be bold. People need hope right now and with God there is more
than hope—there is promise. There is Jesus. For our sake as we live
in this world, for their sakes as they search for security and answers
and new life, and for His sake as His heart longs for them to know.
Let them know. Be still and know.

We are very blessed to live at a time when our White House, our
government and our military are filled for the most part with a very
prayerful people. But with all of this in place, we have no hope if the
people of this nation are not also holding fast to God. When you feel
you can do nothing, ask God to be with those hurting; to gird up our
President with perfect, unselfish wisdom, courage and mercy; to heal a
broken home or to lift our children sky-high; to protect our land and to

pull the nations together in understanding. Ask Him to be the Light of this entire world . . . and you have done everything.

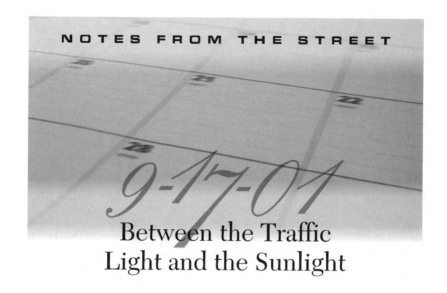

Between the Traffic Light and the Sunlight

9-17-01

Today, New York went back to work, together, and I don't think we've ever understood the word "together" more clearly.

There were lines wrapped around the entire block of the Empire State Building. It was the first day back for those who work there. Only the Fifth Avenue entrance was open and everyone was being checked—thoroughly. As I passed the 34th Street line on my way to work, I heard the faithful talking. An hour's wait to get to work is no skin off their nose if it means an inch closer to safety.

A post-9-11 sigh is still the most common tone of voice, but city sounds are slowly coming back. Traffic is running normally in midtown; even the commercial airlines are flying again—lower than usual though, which sets everyone on pins and needles. One of the landing patterns runs right over the island—always has—but the sound is now unwelcome. It's too fresh for most.

At work, every phone call or e-mail is prefaced by well wishes and condolences. Every so often you check out CNN to see what kind of tricks the stock market is going to do on its first day back in town.

The caravans of sirens continue down 34th Street almost nonstop and there is still a police presence on every major corner. But this is life as I've become used to it since last week's very solemn Tuesday. What was new for me and for most other New Yorkers came with a trip downtown on the train.

I wasn't sure where the train was going to stop. The lowest Manhattan had been open yet was Canal Street. Now, I'd heard it was running all the way to Wall Street but I wasn't sure if that was literal (Wall Street Station) or if it meant the Wall Street area. So I got edgy and jumped out at City Hall, a taboo world where, for the first time since everything had changed, you didn't need a city badge to enter. I took a picture of the Brooklyn Bridge with no traffic. World Trade Center signs were missing but makeshift Triage signs remained, in particular a pink sheet of scrap paper taped to a phone booth pointing the injured and their heroes toward the impromptu Triage center at Pace University.

On the corner of Park Row, two Marines sat on an upturned milk crate—one with a cup of Starbucks and the other with a pack of Oreos. I thought, "So this is what war looks like in America . . . Starbucks and Oreos." They were even laughing now and then. But when I noticed the eerily associated ad on the bus stop in front of them (for the television miniseries *Band of Brothers* about a troop of marines) I remembered the citizens they were here to save—some perhaps still waiting, trapped only blocks away.

The sun seemed unusually bright, warm, strong. But it hit me instantly why the sun would seem so foreign in this part of town. It has never shone here at this hour before. The spot where I was standing would usually be directly in the shadow of the towers—but they no longer exist. I've wished for more sunshine in the city for so long, but I never wanted it to come in this way.

Before I moved on, I stopped to read a missing sign on the street corner. All week I've been reading the names and last known locations of those missing, but this was a new one. It read, "Does anyone know of any pets whose people are missing?" The Parks Department, which has been shuttling residents in to retrieve their pets, suddenly realized that there are pets that no one is looking for, since their *owners* have not yet been found. Above the sign someone had written, in small letters with a black magic marker, "Repent." That would be a good idea.

A city bus came through the barricades. No longer used for rush hour commutes, this bus had "Fire Department" and "The Bravest . . . #13" written out in masking tape in the front and side windows. Unmarked SUVs have "NYPD" written in soap on their windows. And we keep making insane remarks like, "I wonder what happened to the pigeons."

On Exchange Street the few shop owners that had come in were sweeping the dust off their doorframes (which reminded me of the Israelites brushing their door frames on the first Passover) and hosing down dust-soaked floor mats. America was cleaning. Better yet, in the surrounding streets, people were (metaphorically speaking) taking hoses and brooms to their lives—being kinder, more patient, more polite and understanding. *Lord, let it last.*

I made it to the end of the street and could see the wreckage for the first time. Even in person it still looks like a movie set. *They're always filming something in this city—why can't this be just a film?* I noticed the burnt red shell of what I assume was building number seven. It looked like nothing but rusted metal—a hundred years old and abandoned.

One block further, as I traversed a circle around Ground Zero (still in the distance but close enough to see with my own eyes for the first time), I saw the image that we probably all saw on the news: the only upright portion of the World Trade Center that remained. It was an uneven, charred, thin edge of what used to be the steel girders at the bottom of the towers. I used to say they looked like tuning forks. I used to stand beneath them and touch the bottom of a beam that continued to impossible heights in the sky. Now it looked like an enlarged version of an old, battered fence on the edge of a farm—a barbed-wire fence that will need repairs when the winter passes. But this will take so much more than repairs. This will take a building of the mettle of this country and our neighbors around the globe—all of them.

And that's the aim. Let's hope we can accomplish it.

Already trying to build morale, the Federal Reserve Bank was pumping brassy patriotic tunes from its first tier into the triangles of the financial district—big-band music, from public loudspeakers halfway up the building that made the strange scene reminiscent of wartime. Between the cobblestone streets, this music and everyone on bicycles to avoid the trains, it seemed I'd either gone fifty years into the past or to another country. Everyone stopped and looked up as they came around the corner as if they suddenly discovered themselves in someone else's life.

The stock exchange had Old Glory blanketed across the front of the building. Must be why it behaved somewhat today, its first day back in business. And for those of you who've seen or visited the large bronze bull in the triangle below Trinity Street, you'll rest easy knowing that D Company 101KF, U.S. Army is posted there, as kind and watchful as you'd hope a good American soldier would be. One block over on Trinity and Exchange, another band of brothers was working above and below ground in tunnels which I'm sure are badly shaken.

ConEd worker Michael McQuoid and his colleagues have become a new kind of hero lately. I'm standing within three blocks of the wreckage now, amidst unbelievable destruction—and yet, strangely, there's a green light shining at the intersection. One green light amidst a blackened war zone. The power's on! He and his colleagues are working on the rest of the district, but what a beautiful, hopeful sight a traffic light can be.

Between the traffic light and the sunlight that shines in new places now, good change is going to come from tough memories. But like New York City did today, we all have a chance to swallow hard and go back to work, together—and this time, harder.

Part 3

All Together Now

In the recent events we seem to have grasped the importance of one another. As families, communities, a nation and a part of the world, we've taken a leap toward understanding that we are here together and that there is a reason for it. Families have been reconciled as a direct result of these events. Organizations and missions with differing goals have joined resources toward the same goal: to heal, to love, to restore. Children from the Midwest gave the money they'd been saving for four years, for their senior trip, to firefighters' families in the New York City area. School children from all over the U.S. wrote to the kids who watched the turmoil from their classroom windows. Children in New York City are writing to children in Israel, Pakistan and Afghanistan, to tell them we love them and we wish for peace. Countries have reached out with letters, memorials and offers of support to tell us we are not alone. In one broadcast, the chancellor of Germany said with passion in the timbre of his voice, "Today, Germany *is* . . . the United States of America."

But there's more to the blessing this understanding brings if we take it past the point of realization and put it into action and achievement. It takes commitment and diligence. We will have to *do* before we feel like doing. We will have to make a decided effort and sacrifice. But when you do these things, almost without noticing you develop an amazing sense of love. It's born out of service, especially when you don't want to serve. It's born out of Christ's heart as He lifts the veil to what He sees.

If we allow Him to adjust our vision to His, to begin to see one another as He sees us, and see His love and sacrifice clearly, we would be as close as it gets to heaven on earth.

Right now we have a chance. More than we've ever realized before, this is our chance to make some dramatic changes. This is not a situation where we can wage a short-lived campaign, leaving the rest to our children's world. In this dire state of affairs, we may have reached the point where, if we don't walk the straight and narrow now, our children will have no chance to fix it; they may not have a free world.

America: stand together, turn to God.

The Uncommon Call

Love one another. . . . Just say your prayers, and maybe God'll help us all out.

—FDNY Captain during interview

While I was writing this book, a fire broke out in the apartment building across the street. Probably something very simple—a kitchen fire or a candle unattended. The fire trucks come often to this neighborhood of old, wooden brownstones, packed side by side. Two or three times a week the trucks are called for one reason or another, often for false alarms.

This one was an actual fire (on the second floor, I later learned), and I'm sure a pretty easy call by comparison. Five floors up, a woman was waving her hands and covering her nose with her sleeve. "Top floors are tough," one of the firemen would later say. "That's where all the smoke goes."

The woman in the window waited, waving her purse, shouting "hello." She never even had to climb out onto the ladder; a fireman came to her instead. He climbed in the window and made things right.

Interesting comparison to God. I am not calling firefighters God; I'm calling us the ones in danger. The comparison is in the seeking. If you call to Him, He's there; if you seek Him, you will find Him. He comes to make things right.

The smoke was billowing from the vent shafts on the roof, filling the upper floors of the building. I sat in my window and watched the

69

men rally with a more gripping sense of gratitude than ever before. It was the first I'd seen fire trucks in general action since the day the whole image of a fire truck changed forever. And, indeed, I saw them and their fellows in a whole new way.

What I noticed most was tenacity. Walking around on a tiny upper Manhattan street I saw the same determination that America is trying to emulate. It is the resolve demonstrated by Lisa Beamer (the widow of Todd Beamer, a passenger on the hijacked flight that crashed in Pennsylvania) when she climbed on that flight from Boston to finish her husband's journey and to encourage us all to go on with ours. These men were no longer just doing their job; they were shining, walking like ten-foot heroes, because they carried a lot more weight than just their gear in order to get the job done.

That was it—I had to talk to them. Grabbing my old blue baseball cap, notepad and shoes, I reached the bottom of the stairs just as they were rolling the hoses up. I met a couple of the greatest guys on in the FDNY—though the more of them I meet, I learn they're all "the greatest."

I introduced myself while standing in the middle of the street behind their truck. I cannot imagine what it must have taken to crush one of these substantial vehicles. And the boys were all comedians. They laughed and apologized for the big dirty glove I was most grateful to shake.

"I'm a mess," said one of the kindest faces.

Gentlemen, we'd all give so much if we were able to share a little of that dust with you—to brush just a little bit of it off of your shoulders and carry it for a while ourselves.

I laughed with a bunch of strangers who were instantly family. They called over a fourth man.

"What—am I in trouble?"

"Yeah, I called the mayor on you."

"Again?" he says.

One of them was sitting on the truck bumper laughing when he accidentally touched his hand to the truck's taillight and pulled it away. "Sheesh . . . hot." We laughed again. Fireman . . . and the taillight's hot. I love these guys.

Lieutenant Andrew Brett, Sean O'Brien, James O'Boyle, Jim Elnendorf . . . when I finished writing down their names and laughing, the lieutenant, probably unknowingly, reminded me with one uneasy glint in his eye that it is hard to keep working; that you have to laugh, but the sorrow's not gone.

"These are the guys," he said, "that were working that day. They all died."

He directed my attention to a handwritten scrawl, in white paint, of first names, all in a row: Glen, Bob, Paul, Joe . . . But as Lieutenant Brett pointed to each one, he said the full name. He didn't have to look it up in a book somewhere; he knew these men. Their names were in his heart. He called them off as his finger followed the list painted on the back of the truck. And I wrote in my little blue notebook, so glad I had taken the time to come down and hear their names spoken in the sound of the lieutenant's voice: Glenn Perry, Bob Minara, Paul Ruback, Joe Rivelli, Matt Barnes, John Collins, Ken Kumpel. I looked up and touched the sign: *"They gave it all."*

These men worked in my neighborhood, at Ladder Company 25. I know exactly where the firehouse is. I could draw you a map. It's on 77th Street—only two blocks up and one block over. So very close.

My car broke down in front of the firehouse one time and a couple of the guys sitting out front pushed it up the street so it was safe by a hotel and I could go home to call a tow truck. But I had never come by just to meet them. Now some of them are gone—maybe even the ones that pushed my car.

How could I reward them now for their lives? Only by honoring their brothers, by changing a few things about the way I live and by actively expressing my gratitude, rather than settling for "good intentions." This brought to mind the Firefighter's Prayer. There are no "good intentions" in their prayer, only solid dedication:

Firefighter's Prayer

When I am called to duty,
Wherever flames may rage,

Give me the strength to save a life
Whatever be its age.

Help me embrace a little child
Before it is too late,
Or save an older person from
The horror of that fate.

Enable me to be alert
And hear the weakest shout,
And quickly and efficiently
To put the fire out.

I want to fill my calling and
To give the best in me,
To guard my every neighbor and
Protect his property.

And if according to God's will
I must answer death's call
Bless with Your protecting hand
My family, one and all.

When you move into a new neighborhood, I encourage you to
find out where the local firehouse is and go there. Introduce yourself
by name and thank them for watching over your home and others.
People with four-year-olds do this already, but it's not against the
rules to go without a kindergartner in tow. If you've got a bit of Mar-
tha Stewart in you, bake them something. Firemen love food.

Then go to the local police precinct and introduce yourself to the
sergeant there. Thank him for leading the men that watch over your
neighborhood. This is not crazy. Believe me, I've spoken to these
men and they will not only understand, they will be grateful.

Why should we do this? Because they're heroes before the tragedy
comes. They do their jobs with just as much heart before the world
changes. Then when it does, and their brothers fall beside them, they

go on that very same day. With no less guts and glory than the bravest American soldier, they go on. They finish the job and are ready at the next.

It's the same principle with God. Don't wait for the tragedy to strike. Go to the "firehouse" in prayer and introduce yourself by name to the One who watches over you, and say thank you. Then do it again every day.

Lord I know You are there, and today, I acknowledge it again. Thank You for being the Strength of those who need You. Thank You for being the Hand that holds me and pulls me from the fire. Thank You that I have enough peace in my soul to know I needn't be afraid, no matter what . . . that I can be still in my heart. I want to get to know You now, not just when the fire threatens and there's danger at my door. Let me know You now.

Sit in the firehouse for a while. Meet God with your heart. Meet the firemen on the corner and have a cup of coffee. Take care of one another. There is a verse that says it is not good for man to be alone. In the context it refers to a man and a woman. But in the constant character of God that He reveals through all the Scriptures, we can see clearly that it also refers to us all being put here together.

We need God in our lives, and yes, we do need one another. Reach out. Take this beyond the firehouse. Take it to your neighbor, the person at the bank window you see once every two weeks, your children's teachers, the friend or stranger that wants to talk when you're so tired.

Get to know them. Find Jesus in this world and take Him to others. He's not hard to find at all.

"Now, Since We're a Family"

Eight

Getting to know one another, depending on one another, reaching out—this spirit is captured in a story that's being circulated about a commercial flight in which the pilot made a moving announcement. It was originally offered as "flight instructions" for the passengers, on the new way to fly.

Indeed, it is a brilliant idea for anyone flying on any airline, at anytime. It will still be a brilliant idea twenty years from now. Friendly skies or terra firma, it's a great spirit to apply to life—no matter where you are, no matter what you're doing.

Aboard Flight 564: What to do if your airplane is hijacked
by Peter Hannaford, Public Affairs Consultant

As it was with most U.S. airports, last Saturday was the first near-normal day at Denver International since the terrorist attacks. On United Airlines Flight 564, the door had just been locked and the plane was about to pull out of the gate when the captain came on the public address system.

"I want to thank you brave folks for coming out today. We don't have any new instructions from the federal government, so from now on we're on our own."

The passengers listened in total silence.

He explained that airport security measures had pretty much solved the problem of firearms being carried aboard, but not weapons of the type the terrorists

75

apparently used, plastic knives or those fashioned from wood or ceramics.

"Sometimes a potential hijacker will announce that he has a bomb. There are no bombs on this aircraft and if someone were to get up and make that claim, don't believe him.

"If someone were to stand up, brandishing something such as a plastic knife and say, 'This is a hijacking,' or words to that effect, here is what you should do: Every one of you should stand up and immediately throw things at that person—pillows, books, magazines, eyeglasses, shoes—anything that will throw him off balance and distract his attention. If he has a confederate or two, do the same with them. Most important: get a blanket over him, then wrestle him to floor and keep him there. We'll land the plane at the nearest airport and the authorities will take it from there.

"Remember, there will be one of him and maybe a few confederates, but there are 200 of you. You can overwhelm them. The Declaration of Independence says, 'We, the people,' and that's just what it is when we're up in the air: we, the people, vs. would-be terrorists. I don't think we are going to have any such problem today or tomorrow or for a while, but sometime down the road it is going to happen again and I want you to know what to do.

"Now, since we're a family for the next few hours, I'll ask you to turn to the person next to you, introduce yourself, tell him a little about yourself and ask him to do the same."

I submit we're not just a family "for the next few hours" on an airplane; we're a family always. And it's very possible that with this undesired wake-up call, we can live like a great family—like God's family.

The story from United Airlines was a good wake-up call for me. Not only is it a little more Christlike than what my first instinct would usually be, but it also gets business done. It provides a safer, more prepared environment—and not only in an airplane, as initially intended. If applied at all times, in our own homes and communities, it provides a safer, more prepared nation. The beauty is that, as we're working on building the columns of our nation for the sake of peace and security, we will discover the kind of relationships God had planned for us to have with one another all along. We will discover what He intended for us to be to one another—family.

Like any family, it will not always be easy. This burst of patriotism and understanding may fade a bit over time. Hopefully, it won't fade completely, but it doesn't have to fade at all if we take the lessons to heart and genuinely learn to live differently. And we must teach our children that different way of life, so that they will make it their task to keep it strong.

It is possible.

"This Is Your
Captain Speaking"

Sure, I pray before a flight—but then, sometimes I forget why I do. I pray before, during and after a flight. Something about being lifted 30,000 feet in the air by strangers in a man-made machine brings people to prayer. But it's more than this—it's the broad possibilities and the knowledge of things that can happen on flights.

Fran Drescher's hit sitcom *The Nanny* was born on an airplane when the passenger list happened to include both her and a well-known producer. People have met their spouses through divinely designed seat assignments. Better still, lives have met Christ through the same "coincidences"—in airplanes, buses, trains, classrooms, the waiting room at the local auto-repair shop. Divine appointments happen all the time and there is always a need to look after your neighbor, to listen for that still, small voice urging you to speak—and to follow that urge, even when it's tough.

I love the fact that God knows this before we even take our seats.

Prior to the events of September 11, evangelist William Faye was boarding a flight. He noticed the flight attendant breaking up a bag of ice by beating it with a bottle. With the rare grace of a gentleman and in the spirit of Christ, he halted what she was doing by saying, "Please don't do that; you'll cut your hand. I care about you."

He's not one to avoid the draw of the Holy Spirit on his heart that seemed to keep saying, "Witness to the flight attendant." It wasn't an unusual experience for him. He travels frequently and there's rarely a day that goes by, no matter where he is, that he doesn't tell someone about his Savior. He read me a few lines from some of the heart-melting letters he's received just in the past few months from those who have boarded a plane alone and found a whole knew life before they landed.

Most of the time, there was nothing that made it easier for him to broach the subject—no one outright asking him about his faith—and there wasn't this time with his new friend and the bottle-turned-ice-pick. It was up to him to bring the love of the Lord to her. The Shepherd had made it clear: "Witness to the flight attendant."

He gave her one of the Cassie Bernall tracts he carries—a testimony about one of the young girls from Columbine. It's a story close to his heart as he was chaplain to the Denver, Colorado Police Department.

He wasn't in his seat more than a minute when she came by and said, "You know, this is weird. You are the sixth person to hand me one of these in the last two weeks. Why did you give this to me?"

You'd be surprised what happens when the authority of the Holy Spirit takes over. I used to expect tongue lashings—loudly, and in public—or losing the chance to get to know someone as he walks away, rolling his eyes and mumbling something about the Bible Belt. Sure, that's not beyond happening, but the Lord writes some amazing stories when we listen and follow His lead. Jesus watched to see where the Father was working. That's all we have to do. But when we see, we must also meet the need:

Faye talked with her in the galley. He prayed with her and led her to Christ.

She was a flight attendant on one of the planes that went down on September 11th.

When the Lord speaks, listen. When the Lord calls, obey. When the Lord says, "Tell the flight attendant I love her," tell the flight attendant. It's not worth the political correctness. It's not worth the nap on a long flight. It's not about us at all. When the Lord leads, tell them.

Carry the Torch

*Let us throw off everything that hinders and the sin that
so easily entangles, and let us run with perseverance the
race marked out for us.* (Hebrews 12:1)

Jeff was a missionary, a teacher, an athlete. He had a great love for
the game of life—the disciplines, the teamwork and running the
race with a fervor. He was about Christ in everything he did, in the
way he lived his life.

On September 11th he was attending a meeting at the Twin
Towers to find the funds to continue his ministry. Nobody quite
knows what happened. The stories are still settling. But he was injured badly and required several surgeries.

Holly, also an athlete at heart, was his girlfriend of many years. He
was about to propose, but she didn't find this out until she read a letter
he had written "in case anything happens." After the towers came
down, Jeff was fighting and healing, first at a New York hospital and
later at one in Stanford, California. Holly had a few good chances in the
meantime to talk with him, and she and I had even made contact
about including Jeff's story among the others in this book. We set up a
time to talk in between her travels to visit him. When I finally called,
she seemed distracted, somber. I asked, "Is now a good time to talk?"

"No," she said almost apologetically. Then in the calmest, most
peaceful tone of voice she told me, "Jeff has passed away."

I didn't know what to say to this stranger for whom I suddenly cared
so much.

It was a week later that we were finally able to connect. I was surprised she still wanted to talk to me. But as she told me her story, and

Jeff's, I knew his passing was a part of the story. It was what brought God's message the most clearly to light.

The calmness and peace in Holly's voice that I had mentioned was one of the first things she spoke of. She called it a *blanket of confidence*.

Since Jeff's passing, only seven days before our interview, she had already had the opportunity to speak at several churches. "It's a hard subject to get through," she said. "It's hard sometimes to think about and talk about, but as I share, I feel a complete sense of calmness—a blanket of confidence."

She began to tell me about Jeff and what she'd already told so many others in his name. He had a dream of going to the Olympics. That dream disappeared with him, but it has given birth to a powerful image of encouragement: the image of a torch proudly carried.

"I think of the Olympic torch and all that it represented: devotion, sacrifice, ambition, anticipation, perseverance, fervor, a focus on excellence. His life and his faith were a torch proudly carried. When he died, it felt for a moment like the torch had been dropped. But as I began to share his story, and saw the lives that were touched and even changed, then I began to see how everyone else had picked it up again.

"In three churches where I spoke just after his funeral, nearly a hundred people came to the altar at each. That was 300 people right there. The wrestling team got together at Jeff's university to pray and to call others to pray, and soon the network had expanded to include over 1,000 people praying. I'm not so quiet about my faith now. We're praying everywhere—on campus, in a restaurant for twenty minutes. It has changed. There are no barriers.

"It has given my life a whole new purpose. I've learned that ministry is about daily life, the little things. It's about investing in people's lives. So invest. Tell them whatever you want to tell them while they're here. Do something simple. Leave them a note. Care.

"It's my job, now, to carry the torch and keep running. And so many people are doing the same thing.

"Like an athlete, you have bad games, you get injured and carrying on is difficult, but you have to give all, all the time. You have to give everything."

The Kindness of Strangers

About five hours out of Frankfurt, Germany flying over the North Atlantic, Nazim-Amin, a Delta Airlines flight attendant, was taking his break in a crew rest seat. No one on the flight at that moment had any idea what was going on across the sea. Until . . .

The curtains parted abruptly and he was summoned to the cockpit to speak with the captain.

"As soon as I got there," Nazim writes, "I noticed that the crew had one of those 'all business' looks on their faces. The captain handed me a printed message and as I quickly looked over it, I realized its importance."

The message had come in from Atlanta. It was addressed by their flight number and read simply, "All airways over the Continental U.S. are closed. Land ASAP at the nearest airport, advise your destination."

Nazim noted that when a dispatcher tells you to land immediately without suggesting an airport, indicating they've relinquished control of the flight to the pilot, one can assume it is a serious situation. They needed to get on the ground immediately.

As Nazim continues his narrative, he takes you into a very intimate setting, a rare personal glimpse at one of those warm and encouraging stories that come out of times of war. It's surreal to realize, as you read the following account, that such a time is now.

"It was quickly calculated that the nearest airport was 400 miles away, behind our right shoulder, in Gander, on the island of Newfoundland. A quick request was made to the Canadian traffic controller and they immediately approved a right turn, directly into Gander.

83

"The in-flight crew was told to get the airplane ready for an immediate landing. Meanwhile, another message arrived from Atlanta telling us about some terrorist activity in the New York area. 'So that's why there was no hesitation by the Canadian controller approving our request . . .'

"We briefed the in-flight crew about going to Gander and we went about our business closing down the airplane for a landing. A few minutes later I went back to the cockpit and found out about the other hijacked airplanes. We decided to make an announcement and lie to the passengers for the time being. We told them that an instrument problem had arisen on the airplane and that we needed to land at Gander to have it checked. We promised to give more information after landing in Gander. There were many unhappy passengers, of course. We landed in Gander about forty minutes after [receiving the first message]."

When they landed, the truth was noticeable. There were already about twenty other airplanes on the ground, from all over the world. The Delta flight parked on the ramp and the captain made the following announcement.

"Ladies and gentlemen, you must be wondering if all these airplanes around us have the same instrument problem we have. The reality is that we are here for a good reason." He went on to explain the little bit they knew at the time about the situation in the United States.

Nazim tells us, "There were loud gasps and stares of disbelief."

Gander control instructed them to stay put. No one was allowed to get off the aircraft. No one on the ground was allowed to come near the aircraft.

Nazim describes a strange, dreamlike scene: "A car from the airport police would come around once in a while, look us over and go on to the next airplane. In the next hour or so all the airways over the North Atlantic were vacated and Gander alone ended up with fifty-three airplanes from all over the world, out of which twenty-seven were flying U.S. flags. We were told that each and every plane was to be offloaded, one at a time, with the foreign carriers given the priority. We were No.

14 in the U.S. category. Our tentatively scheduled time to deplane was 6 p.m."

Local time at Gander was half past noon. In New York City, it was a fresh and stunned 11 a.m. They would sit and wait on the plane at least six hours, while in the States, the mayhem continued.

While they spent the day on the plane, bits of information started to come in over the aircraft radio. Together in their new tight-knit, ten-seat-wide community, they digested the news.

By late in the evening the reports had filtered in that the World Trade Center buildings had collapsed, the Pentagon had also been hit by a plane and that a fourth hijacking had resulted in a crash.

Nazim said, "Now the passengers were totally bewildered and emotionally exhausted, but stayed calm as we kept reminding them to look around to see that we were not the only ones in this predicament. There were fifty-two other planes with people on them in the same situation. We told them that the Canadian government was in charge and we were at their mercy; there was nothing we could do to make any of it move any faster."

He acknowledged that those in charge were in an unprecedented situation and were handling it to the best of their ability. Nonetheless, it was understandably difficult when the news came in at 6 p.m.—originally their scheduled time to deplane—that they wouldn't get their turn to do so until 11 a.m. the next morning. They would be on the plane an additional seventeen hours. Counting time both on the ground and in the air, they would then have been on the plane well over a day.

"That took the last wind out of the passengers," Nazim said. He mentioned only the others' feelings, never what he felt personally. It showed me his mind-set of service was still active at this time.

He continued, "They simply resigned and accepted this news without much noise and settled into a mode of preparing to spend the night on the airplane. Gander had promised us any and all medical attention if needed—medicine, water, lavatory servicing. And they were true to their word. Fortunately, we had no medical situation during the night. We did have a young lady who was thirty-three weeks into her preg-

nancy. We took really good care of her. The night passed without any
further complications on our airplane despite the uncomfortable sleeping arrangements."

About 10:30 on the morning of the 12th, they were finally told to
get ready to leave the aircraft. A convoy of school buses came up
alongside the airplane; the stairway was hooked up and the passengers were taken to the terminal for "processing."

The crew was taken to the same terminal but told to go to a different section, where they were processed through immigration and
customs and then had to register with the Red Cross. They were
then isolated from their passengers and taken in a caravan of vans to
a very small hotel in the town of Gander.

"We had no idea where our passengers were going," Nazim said, still
showing concern for the welfare of others. "The town of Gander has a
population of 10,400 people. The Red Cross told us that they were going to process about 10,500 passengers from all the airplanes that were
forced into Gander. We were told to relax at the hotel and wait for a
call to go back to the airport, but not to expect that call for a while."

It wasn't until they got to their hotels and turned on the TV that passengers and crew were struck with the total scope of the terror back
home. It had already been over twenty-four hours since it had all begun.

Nazim said he and the crew kept themselves amused by "going
around town, discovering things and enjoying the hospitality. The
people were so friendly. They knew that we were the 'plane people'
and they took such kind care of all of us.

"We all had a great time while we waited for our call, which came
two days later on September 14 at 7 a.m. We made it to the airport
by 8:30 a.m. and departed for Atlanta at half past noon—exactly
three days after we first touched down in Gander, Newfoundland."
They touched down in Atlanta at 4:30 that afternoon.

During the flight to Atlanta, the passengers had a chance to share
with the crew details of their wonderful experiences, and the enchanting sentiment between the people of Gander and their new visitors.

Under such somber global conditions, it was an almost fairy-tale meeting of two divergent worlds.

"Gander and the surrounding small communities, within a seventy-five kilometer radius, had closed all the high schools, meeting halls, lodges and any other large gathering places," Nazim reported. "They converted all these facilities to mass lodging areas. Some had cots set up, some had mats with sleeping bags and pillows. All the high school students were asked to volunteer to take care of the 'guests.'

"The passengers from this flight ended up in a town called Lewisporte, about forty-five kilometers from Gander. There they were given a place to stay in a high school. If any women wanted to be in a women-only facility, that was arranged. Families were kept together. All the elderly passengers were taken to private homes.

"The young pregnant woman was put up in a private home right across the street from a twenty-four-hour urgent care type facility.

"There were medical personnel on call and they had both male and female nurses available who stayed with the crowd for the duration.

"Phone calls and e-mails to the U.S. and Europe were available for everyone once a day. During the days the passengers were given a choice of 'excursion trips.' Some people went on boat cruises of the lakes and harbors. Some went to see the local forests.

"Food was prepared by all the residents and brought to the school for those who elected to stay put. Others were driven to the eatery of their choice and fed. Local bakeries stayed open to make fresh bread for the guests.

"Everyone was given tokens to go to the local Laundromat to wash their clothes, since their luggage was still on the aircraft.

"In other words, every single need was met."

Nazim recalls, "Passengers were crying while telling us these stories. After all that, they were delivered to the airport right on time and without a single one missing or late. All because the local Red Cross had all the information about the goings-on back at Gander and knew which group needed to leave for the airport at what time. Absolutely incredible.

"When passengers came on board, it was like they had been on a cruise together. Everybody knew everybody else by name. They were swapping stories of their stay, impressing each other with who had the better time. It was mind-boggling. Our flight back to Atlanta looked like a party flight. We simply stayed out of their way. The passengers had totally bonded and they were calling each other by their first names, exchanging phone numbers, addresses and e-mail addresses. And then a strange thing happened. . . .

"One of our business class passengers approached me and asked if he could speak over the P.A. to his fellow passengers. We never, never allow that. But something told me it was important. I said 'of course.' The gentleman picked up the microphone and reminded everyone about what they had just gone through in the last few days. He reminded them of the hospitality they had received at the hands of total strangers. He further stated that he would like to do something in return for the good folks of the town of Lewisporte.

"He said he was going to set up a trust fund under the name of *DELTA 15* (our flight number). The purpose of the trust fund would be to provide scholarships for the high school students of Lewisporte to help them go to college.

"He asked for donations of any amount from his fellow travelers. When the paper with donations got back to us with the amounts, names, phone numbers and addresses, it totaled to $14,500 or about $20,000 Canadian. The gentleman who started all this turned out to be an M.D. from Virginia. He promised to match the donations and to start the administrative work on the scholarship. He also said that he would forward this proposal to Delta Corporate and ask them to donate as well.

"Why all of this?" Nazim concludes. "Just because some people in faraway places were kind to some strangers, who happened to literally drop in among them."

9-18-01

Happy Anniversary?

*J*ust like any morning lately, I awoke and felt a realization coming on. It greets you every day, gently but unavoidably, and as close as the sun through the window. "I'm sorry," it says, "I hate to do this to you, but I'm real."

In the rush to leave, I'd almost put it behind me for a moment, but when I sat to tie my shoes the 1010 WINS news reporter came on in a wearied voice and said, "It's almost here, folks. In one minute, we reach the anniversary of the moment it all began. At 8:48 last Tuesday, a plane hit the north tower of the World Trade Center. It has been, folks, one week this minute." The WINS news tone sounded and the bells of St. Patrick's began to toll.

One week? How can it have been a week? How can something so constant, so non-singular, have an anniversary?

I sighed and hung my head with only one shoe tied. If I keep this minute of silence, I'll be late. But I can't seem to get back to my shoe.

A coworker I met on the train made me pause with him as we passed 5th Avenue. I had never noticed the view of the WTC from there, but he had—every morning—and described in detail how he

89

remembered them off to the right of the Flatiron building. It was like being at a memorial service for a loved one and hearing a stranger describe something you'd never known about that person.

At work, people periodically crept into my office to check on the Empire State Building—what the firemen were up to, how the surroundings were doing and generally just making sure it was still there.

The local news talk was still very shell-shocked and hurt. You can hear the raw emotion in the newscasters' voices. Now that a week has passed, the joke is up, right? It never really happened. It was all just a test. Did we pass?

But it did happen, and Morry Alter, channel 2 news (CBS), began a week in review by telling us where we were last Tuesday morning: "We were all somewhere doing something that was about to mean nothing in the scheme of things." Before he closed his report, he did lift New York up again, building spirits with our advances. "We're doing just fine today," he said. "We've sold some stocks, we've played some ball. We're doing just fine today." And one day at a time is about at far as anyone wants to take it.

On this, my city's anniversary, I had to go home for the night. I couldn't go back downtown. I will again tomorrow and see where the boundaries have moved, how people's spirits have changed, what businesses have opened. Meanwhile, there are plenty of images left over from my last trip downtown, like, for instance, the stories that Dust can tell.

That's capitalized on purpose because this is not just any dust. I filled an empty film canister with telltale dust of the aftermath. I scooped it from the back edge of a phone booth. If I'd been thinking more clearly, I'd have gathered much more. This is not a souvenir, mind you, not a commercial interest. It's a humble and solemn interest, an attempt to keep something near and remember it—both what happened and what caused it—so that I can do my small part to make sure it never happens again.

The consistency actually shocked me. It wasn't dense or grainy like sand. Nor was it light or powdery like ash that disintegrates when touched. It was a completely foreign feel, a sturdy dust collection that you could make into flakes of paper if you pressed it between your fingers. But when you rubbed your fingers together it was as soft as silk and it coated everything in a fine, gauzy layer. It's barely describable. I guess it's a mistake to assume any part of this event would be common.

It wasn't just how the dust felt; it was where you could find it. One exact half of the scaffolding poles were covered about a tenth of an inch in gray. The opposing half was clean as a whistle. It was the same way the whole way down the row. It showed direction. It proved that what you tried to think was a movie, was real; that just as every clip had shown, the cloud really had blown in one direction down the street. And it stuck with force to every surface in its way.

In the front windows of Godiva Chocolates, extravagant tins and truffles sat covered with dust so thick you almost couldn't read "Godiva" on the lid. It was like I'd discovered a lost city.

And have you wondered what became of the street vendors' carts? They're still there, marked in yellow wax pen with the location where they were found. One cart pushed aside read, "corner of Trinity & Exchange." It was full of dusty donuts. A hilarious sight, until I wondered if anyone would be coming back for this cart. Who was the donut man that morning and where is he now?

This also emphasized what an inclusive job the volunteers and service people had done in cleaning house. Details like the famous bronze bull I mentioned earlier. Who dusted off the bull? It was absolutely polished.

One-liners came in through e-mails all day long. After hearing further reports of a backlash against Arab citizens and Islamic mosques, Richard Schneider, senior staff editor and writer for *Guideposts* Magazine, wrote, "It reminds me of when hoodlums tried to hang my grandfather in Chicago during World War I." A poignant and removed description to grab our attention under very highly charged circumstances.

Joyce Hart from Hartline Marketing e-mailed me the lyrics to the old song, 'Through It All,' to remind me how I can learn trust from such an abysmal situation. Wonderfully, when I think of this song, I hear it sung in my father's voice:

> There've been many tears and sorrows, I've had
>   questions for tomorrow.
> There were times I didn't know right from wrong.
> But in every situation, God gave blessed consolation.
> Jesus let me know that I was His own.
> Through it all, through it all, I've learned to trust in
>   Jesus, I've learned to trust in God.
> Through it all, through it all, I've learned to
>   depend upon His Word.

People are taking this time to reach out, to do, to tell their story and share their thoughts. Even my dad is writing "parables" now! I don't remember the last time my dad wrote such a thing, but he sent me an e-mail about the roots threatening his backyard pool. I saw them myself on a recent visit—thick as a thumb running twenty feet underground. You can't get to them; you can just see their lingering potential for serious damage under the vinyl lining. So what do you do? Remove the source.

That's what we must do to battle the danger to us now. With the unseen threat of terrorist forces, our President and those surrounding him know they must remove the source, and the aggressive roots will be incapacitated. There is a positive, enabling version of this illustration in Christ's parable of the vine and the branches. "I am the vine, you are the branches. If a man remains in me and I in him, he will bear much fruit; apart from me, you can do nothing" (John 15:5). Apart from Him, we wither.

I urge you, no matter where you live, to do something. It can be a very small thing—sharing a word of encouragement, displaying a confidence of faith that others can lean on, offering up a prayer. We've known in our heads for years the multiplication possibilities of small-boat, big-sea efforts. But there's no more time for waiting. We have to learn it in our guts and go. If a mustard seed of faith can move a mountain, it can move God's hand around the globe.

Just ten days ago, I was in California where my mother was praising the gorgeous day from the passenger-side window as we drove to Grass Valley. And it was, too. Perfect, untouched, glorious. Then, with a sound of gratefulness, she said (whether to my father and I, to herself, to God or to all of the above), "You never know how long you're going to be here."

No, we don't. Nor how long others will be here. Nor how long life will feel the same—glorious and untouched in the lingering warmth of summer. But America didn't fall apart this week—America just grew up a little. Now we've got to decide to what end we're going to use our lives, and just who our country is going to be.

Part 4

Stars and Stripes Forever

Battered to Be Made Whole

There was a beautifully arresting image playing against the sky at the first game of the 2001 World Series tonight. There, in the house that Ruth built, the same place where the world had recently gathered for a joint memorial service, was a broken flag.

It looked like a piece from history, something left over from the Civil War, something that should be in a museum (and probably some day will be). But this flag was new. It had flown at the World Trade Center, at Ground Zero. It was the flag our heroes hoisted above the rubble, to "give proof through the night." Battered and torn, it had a gaping hole in the middle.

It was stunning. I couldn't help but see the Savior, reminding us again of how He had been broken to make us whole. With every wave, the story shone fresh again. It did indeed give proof through the night that not only was our flag still there, but also that God was still there.

A defeated people wouldn't have been able to bear looking at that flag. But with joy at the opportunity to define hope, strength and glory for all the world, we Americans hoisted that tattered flag up on a pole to tell the story.

And in the background, we played baseball. We are so *not* defeated that, within sight of a national tragedy, we get together on a weeknight to play some ball. Well, God bless America.

I don't recognize this strange new world I live in, but I do have great hope that it's the kind of world I've longed for.

We've all gone back to school to try to figure out our national identity and what it is exactly that we choose to pledge allegiance to. We're passing around quotes from former Presidents and leaders that suddenly make so much more sense as we learn firsthand the value of national duty and worth. We're living in uncharted territory, trying to find the balance between genuine loyalty and super-patriotic fad. There are new flames burning inwardly and outwardly, passion directed both at the "evildoers" and at our own home front.

I now understand Veteran's Day and Memorial Day more than ever. I understand gratitude, now that I've learned in my gut that it's not a given for our skies to be free and our land to be safe. I have watched an empty American sky, dotted only with the stark silhouette of a single F-16. As it passed I saluted every man and woman that ever put their life on the line for God-given freedom, and I pledge to do my part, to hold to God, to serve my brothers and sisters of all faiths and nations, to build up and not tear down, to stand in faith. That's my pledge of allegiance and I gladly lend it to the identity of the flag.

I know that in the end, we're accountable only for our own resolve, but valor begets valor. The decisions we make and the people we are does have an effect on what others will be moved to do or to become. I have been inspired and stirred to action by the determination and example of others. The nation we are can call the world to glory.

I've been wondering where the Martin Luther Kings and Abraham Lincolns all went. Now, I believe, they're coming. . . .

Waving "New" Glory

"The Stars and Stripes Forever"? To hear it again and again delivered in such random moments brought me to think about the flag. Why do we pledge allegiance to the flag? It's not the banner itself—it's what it stands for. There is so much symbolism in our flag, so much history. Soak it in. Take a look at it. You can't miss it nowadays.

I admit I took part in our spontaneously becoming the banner-boomer generation—all of us. I have two in my office, a little one stuck in a plant and a large, fabric one draped across my door. On the first day back to work after we'd been "hit," I looked everywhere for a flag but the store was sold out and the street vendors hadn't caught on yet. So on the way home, I stopped at a stationery store and bought a leftover plastic Fourth of July tablecloth to hang out my fifth story window. It stuck to my plants.

But all of this was not for sensationalism, jumping on the band-wagon, being a part of the club or the compulsion to spend on the latest trend. This, to me, is comfort—a constant, visible reminder of what this nation is, was and could be: my flag, my country, which still calls itself one nation under God. The "red, white and blue" carries so many stories of both past and future, of history and promise. It packs a powerful punch to truly observe the flag.

Nearly a year before the September 11th events, I was unknowingly ahead of the game in considering these things when, one afternoon, Old Glory caught me by surprise, pledging its own allegiance to God.

It was a New York City Christmas—a world around me with little lights appearing and celebrations commencing. New York is proud

97

of its holiday season. People walk a bit quicker (as if we don't already fly down the street) and certainly a bit taller. We announce with giddiness that this year's Rockefeller Center tree has been found somewhere, usually just upstate. Hearts begin to open toward missions and needs in the way that they always should be, but which, for some reason, only reaches the proper pinnacle at this time of year.

I walked into the Hyatt on the Avenue of the Americas. I was there to attend the Salvation Army Christmas Luncheon. The spotlights were ballyhooing, the Army band was playing, the curtains were a bright and brilliant red. Sitting quietly in my seat, I was still going a mile a minute on the inside, but then I instantly switched to slow motion as the Spirit began to whisper a gift for the day.

He called my attention with a spotlight and the American flag. The light swung to a corner of the ballroom and caught a shining golden eagle leading yards of red and white and a bold, royal corner of blue. Such majesty—I think I gasped.

The flag was not an uncommon sight, even then, but with the hotly contested presidential election we were enduring at that time (December 2000), it was a clear reminder that the battle for our country has always been much more spiritual than electoral. Little did I know at the time the degree to which the electoral chaos was in fact the spiritual world already in battle, gearing up for the time to come. You could assume just by the way God works that there was some incredible reason, but even with imagination, I couldn't have conceived of what we've now actually seen. For a moment, then, looking at the flag so honorably presented, I felt it.

An unbidden prayer slipped out: "*Oh Lord, make us Yours again.*" So much wrong has been done under that flag—and yet, there has been grace beneath it, too. I realized that we have been His all along and it's never God who has left us, but always we who need to return.

What the flag has experienced in carrying America's name and spirit has also colored it.

It begins with an eagle—a golden, shining eagle atop the pole. "But they that wait upon the LORD shall renew their strength; they shall mount up with wings as eagles" (Isaiah 40:31, KJV). When

America has been weak or wrong, there has been His spirit to heal us, bless us, change us. "But for you who revere my name, the sun of righteousness will rise with healing in its wings" (Malachi 4:2).

Then Old Glory below the eagle—the Stars and Stripes. Red as the stripes on the back of the Messiah, the marks of sins He never committed; red as the blood that was shed in greatest love to save the lives of His children; white as the freedom and redemption His love bought.

And the stars—perhaps the stars He holds in His right hand. Perhaps *the* star that shone above Bethlehem that decorated the sky on a glorious and silencing Noël. The birth of a Savior, the giving of the greatest, most holy and purely loving gift: the giving of Jesus from the hands of God.

They are the hands that put the stars in place at the moment of creation, the hands that held a Savior to a cross at the moment of salvation. And they are the hands that will be waiting at the moment of redemption—open as wide as east and west—waiting to grasp His children to His heart and claim, "I've loved you so, I've loved you so, I've loved you so."

He who holds the stars has spread them across the width of the night sky, and the corner of our flag reflects the glory of the heavens.

Thank You, Lord, for whispering these thoughts as they marched Old Glory in, and for a land where I can stand and sing Your praises. In this constant dialogue You offer, Lord, let us hear and be grateful. Let us comprehend Your nearness—the absolute Creator whispering into the hours of a finite day the wisdom of an infinite universe and the love of a limitless and almighty heart.

Keeping the Spirit
that Flies the Flag

Recently a cartoonist lecturing at a college campus said if you already owned a flag before the attacks, "cool." But if after the attacks you went out and bought a bunch of patriotic tokens, "you should be ashamed of yourself." That's like saying if you had never prayed before, you should be ashamed of turning to God on September 11th—and that's a deplorable fallacy.

I do understand the concern for false patriotism, unreliable reform, short-lived change. But let's not discourage one another from improving ourselves, our families, our nation. Some people who went out and bought their "first" flag did so because they realized what they had taken for granted. For many, this day was a wake-up call. It seems inappropriate to criticize them.

There is an image of what America can be—so much better than it is today—that most people would call impossible. But it is *not* impossible, and when you hear a voice that tells you it is, remember there are two voices and two sources of intent.

One voice belongs to God, who says in His Word: "All things are possible with Christ." If you don't believe this truth, then ask Him with a genuine heart to *show* you. He's promised that He will.

But there is another voice of evil which opposes God. My mother used to say, "Satan is alive and well," and, Scripture adds, "roaming . . back and forth in [the earth]" (Job 2:2). Satan is not just a bold and visible evil, he often works strongest as an undetectable influence. He lies, plain and simple. And the quiet lies of Satan will kill just as surely and quickly as the loudest evil. His subtle lies can disintegrate hope from

101

the inside out. Our nation would suffer the same demise were it not for the sustained mercy of God.

Visiting the *Guideposts* offices in Carmel, New York, I walked through the wide-open parking lot at the top of Seminary Hill. Every single car jutting from its compact space was dressed in some way for what seemed like "USA Day." Windows had those new plastic flag mounts, bumpers had stickers, dashboards had hats lined up like a display-case window.

When I found myself at a standstill, I sighed at the knowledge that this wouldn't last forever, not to this degree. But then that's OK. Someday not every car is going to have a flag, but *every* car doesn't need a plastic flag. What we need to keep is the *spirit* that flies the flag. In this spirit, the red, white and blue will still decorate the countryside, but it will decorate the decorum of the country and shine a light into the world in a much more dramatic way. There will be a moral and good honor to which to pledge allegiance. And *that* would be something to fly.

Our nation's leaders used to be the most rousing inspirers toward remembering that God holds our country. Presidential speeches even as recent as twenty years ago acknowledged the certainties of God's providence and our continual need to be aware of our national relationship with Him. Now that we have been brought through tragedy such as this, a pressure under which people have truly discovered who they are and who we are together, our leaders have once again found their divine responsibility. I am very proud to say they have responded with humility, reverence, resolve and faith.

One example of this was observed in the rotunda of the Capitol on December 4, 2001. In late November the House of Representatives passed a bipartisan resolution providing for a National Day of Reconciliation. Before it was passed, House Majority Whip Tom DeLay delivered a heartfelt statement in favor of the resolution. It is excerpted here:

> We have seldom seen a time in which it would have
> been more fitting than the present moment for America's

leaders to come together as a unified body before God and demonstrate that we seek grace, guidance, wisdom and reconciliation for our nation.

In the work ahead, the old labels and divisions over which we have quarreled must be set aside to accomplish the larger purpose to which we are called as a nation. We believe that this resolution has the capacity to draw us together and to cultivate the meaning, direction and inspiration needed to achieve our special potential in the destiny of nations.

So many of us have gathered meaning and direction for our own lives through the power of prayer. Both Houses of Congress acknowledge this by beginning each legislative day with an invocation. We started work on this resolution many months ago. We were looking for a way to reconcile our country. Recent events have only deepened our conviction that reconciliation is needed and necessary. In the wake of September 11, the imperative underlying a Day of Reconciliation takes on a heightened sense of urgency and weight.

In the past, the American governments have responded to periods of danger and uncertainty by seeking God's blessing and forgiveness. One of our greatest presidents healed a horrible national wound by leading us toward the pathway to reconciliation. He explained that, by embracing our founding principles and seeking God's blessings, our nation could overcome a great crisis. Abraham Lincoln held the nation to account in 1863 as he urged Americans to reflect on all we had inherited and what was expected of us:

> We have been the recipients of the choicest bounties of heaven. We have been preserved, these many years, in peace and prosperity. We have grown in numbers, wealth and power, as no other nation has ever grown. But we have forgotten God.

We have forgotten the gracious hand which preserved us in peace, and multiplied and enriched and strengthened us; and we have vainly imagined, in the deceitfulness of our hearts, that all these blessings were produced by some superior wisdom and virtue of our own.

Intoxicated with unbroken success, we have become too self-sufficient to feel the necessity of redeeming and reserving grace, too proud to pray to God thus!

It behooves us, then, to humble ourselves before the offended Power, to confess our national sins and pray for clemency and forgiveness. If we want America to be united under the fellowship of reconciliation, we must humble ourselves before God and ask to be healed and brought together.

The resolution was passed the same day.

This Land Was Made for You and Me

This country was founded on uncontainable hopes and dreams. This country was founded on faith and dedication. This country was founded on bended knee and by the stable hand of God that blesses our countryside in ways we have nationally forgotten.

I was driving through the lower Hudson Valley with a friend the day the "fighting back" commenced. We had been watching the televised images of the vast Afghani wastelands—a devastating terrain. After a couple hours of war reporting on CNN, it was time for a drive.

My friend and I headed to some of the most beautiful areas of Dutchess County. I had recently discovered some new pockets of gorgeous land, places I knew he hadn't yet been, so that's where I aimed the car. The beauty was astounding.

On an unusually crisp October day we drove slowly across Quaker Hill and beheld the land God allows us. We silently watched flocks of fat pheasants from several different places. There was a flock in someone's front yard on Strawberry Hill. There was another in a small black-fenced field with a few horses and one lone doe who had leapt the fence to visit. Orchards and green rolling hills stretched farther than it was possible to see. On one corner farm there was even the oddity of a two-ton bull in a pasture filled with sheep, reminding me of the biblical portrait of the lamb lying down beside the lion.

There was a spirit of peace and protection in the leaves, sweeping around the edges of stable old homes that had been on those hills for a hundred years. "You know," my friend said, "America doesn't have to look like this. It's not a given. This could just as easily turn to wasteland. But God's hand remains." So somewhere along that two-lane

105

route we pulled over and prayed with our eyes open, gazing out the windows with a thankful tear in our eyes.

Thank You, Lord, that Your hand touches this land, this entire country. Thank You very simply that the whole design still works like it does, that food grows from the ground and rain falls and that all of this is done so beautifully. You feed our bodies, but in the same way You feed our souls with the beauty of it—a beauty in every shape and shade that only one divine Character knows how to create, the secret of perfection in the absolutely patternless.

Forgive us that when You provide out of deep love and Lordship, we not only take it for granted, but we also sometimes ignore and even deny what You've done for our nation. Forgive us, and hold Your hand across our land.

It seems like such a plain prayer, but the other option would be to stay silent, and I would much more readily ask: *Father, bless the earth with food and health. Bless our waters and our soil and all that inhabits it. Make the message clear, tell us again so we can all see that You gave us this land and Your name to enrich it, and that these resources are Yours. Teach us to do right by it and within it.*

> While the storm clouds gather far across the sea,
>   Let us swear allegiance to a land that's free,
> Let us all be grateful for a land so fair,
>   As we raise our voices in a solemn prayer.

That's the prelude to "God Bless America." These last few weeks, after a global wake-up call, it seems we've unofficially made it our new national anthem. Sing it, speak it, hold it in your heart. But put the comma in it: God, bless America. Don't let the message become a general salutation like "have a nice day." Put the comma in it and turn it into a prayer—a direct exchange between you and God. He hears every whisper of the heart. Every time.

God, bless my family; bless those hurting and rebuilding; bless those who are looking for You; answer their call. Bless all Your children, Lord. Bless everyone with the promise of Your own hands to hold them.

And God, please bless America.

God bless America, Land that I love.
　　Stand beside her, and guide her,
Through the night with the light from above.
　　From the mountains, to the prairies, to the oceans
　　　　white with foam.
God bless America, my home sweet home . . .

Just as it is repeated in the song, may we in life repeat it, and not as a lyric but as a prayer.

God bless America, my home sweet home.

Greater Love

To serve the present age,
my calling to fulfill.
Oh may it all my powers engage
to do my Master's will.

> —from "A Charge to Keep," the hymn
> that titles George W. Bush's biography

Our President writes, "I recently received a touching letter that says a lot about the state of America in these difficult times—a letter from a 4th grade girl, with a father in the military. 'As much as I don't want my dad to fight,' she wrote, 'I'm willing to give him to you.' "

Responding to the little girl's letter, President Bush said, "This is a precious gift, the greatest she could give. This young girl knows what America is all about. Since September 11, an entire generation of young Americans has gained a new understanding of the value of freedom and its cost in duty and in sacrifice. The battle is now joined on many fronts. We will not waver; we will not tire; we will not falter; and we will not fail.

"Peace and freedom will prevail."

Thank you and bless you, Mr. President.

This little girl is my hero. She is just one among so many new heroes: the firefighters and rescue workers, the families who have faced jarring losses yet have become an example of grace and strength to the country they love. Thank you, all, for being the toughest threads in the nation's fabric.

That could be the definition of America, the definition of our time, the definition of a people. Our country is far from being perfect. We are not "righteous," for there are "none righteous, no, not one" (Romans 3:10, KJV). But Jesus didn't choose the perfect to be entrusted with the greatest message. He didn't choose the perfect to minister and heal and spread the gospel. He didn't even choose the perfect for His own family bloodline. All of these things are peopled by the most motley crew of all-too-human human beings. And most of the time, that's us.

Yet this country keeps finding eras of people to restore the dream that is American character. I say "eras" and not "generation" because it takes all generations working together—from the little girl mentioned above to senior citizens—whose experience and wisdom are a national treasury. History may have found its next era, but that will be rooted in the choices we make.

As we honor our heroes with what we choose to become, may we also honor the greatest Hero: He who saved the most uncountable number of lives—Jesus Christ.

"Greater love has no one than this, that he lay down his life for his friends" (John 15:13). Greater love has no man than Jesus Christ. Let's make America a country of "greater love."

For our soldiers who are away from home, for the families who let them go, for those in any capacity making sacrifices to fight for divine freedom of God-given rights, I leave you words from an American president:

> I now leave, not knowing when or whether ever I may return, with a task before me greater than that which rested upon Washington. Without the assistance of that Divine Being who ever attended him, I cannot succeed. With that assistance I cannot fail. Trusting in Him who can go with me, and remain with you, and be everywhere for good, let us confidently hope that all will yet be well.

—Abraham Lincoln,
Farewell Address at Springfield
February 11, 1861

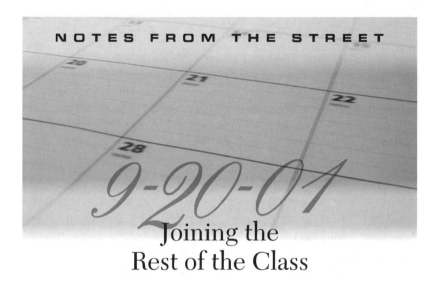

9-20-01
Joining the
Rest of the Class

Since September 11th the world has been dealing with all the effects of post-trauma life in all our individual ways. It's not just our country—it's everyone, everywhere. There is no one who was untouched by last week's events, who isn't dealing with the emotions, tensions and aftermath, and who isn't wondering, just like the rest of us, what's going to happen now.

But in one place—one spot on the planet—it's been just a little bit different. While feeling all the same troubled emotions that the rest of the world is sorting through, here in NYC we were also dealing face-to-face with the local fallout. It's like living through two inconceivable tragedies at once. If you live outside of New York, imagine adding every conflicting, perplexing emotion you've felt in the last ten days to the daily burden of a visible reminder . . . in person. Imagine living in Seattle and looking at the crumbling remains of the Needle for days, or in St. Louis, where blackened pieces of the Arch litter the city. Or imagine San Francisco is your heart's long-time home, and you sit and watch from your pastel townhouse as the Golden Gate smolders, devastated in the bay. And add to any of these the reality of thousands of lives lost, their families your neighbors, and a global unrest unleashed.

There is a stunning presence missing from this city—a massive daily image, gone. Two friends of mine, returning home from a trip, described the hollow ache one felt for the very first time on the turnpike without the city's twin crown shining in the horizon. Our welcome sign is missing, our mighty North Star. We mapped our paths by those buildings and even when we didn't, we couldn't miss the sense of steel sensibility standing sentinel at the Hudson Bay.

I heard a passerby say the same, that very first night when no one really believed it yet. I had packed a bag to visit a friend in midtown because I couldn't imagine sleeping in an empty apartment when the rest of the world was gripping each other's forearms to steady their shock. I flung my bag—laptop, camera and all—over my shoulder and headed to church on foot (I must admit I was too unnerved to walk to 42nd Street alone). Making the curve around Columbus Circle I heard a college kid say to his buddies, "I can't believe they're gone . . . how'm I supposed to find my way around the village?" They laughed together, but it was a nervous laughter—very nervous.

There was more laughter on the 12th when I asked the storekeepers for a paper. "Are you kidding?" they smiled. There wasn't a single paper to be had—not even the *Post*; only a late-release special issue around noon. I dragged my big bag around Times Square trying to figure out what one does on such a day—"the morning after." The offices were closed. I bought a stack of postcards, a few cheap T-shirts—anything that featured the WTC. These things were already fading—any proof of the towers' existence seeping out into a world of shoeboxes, diaries, packed away as visual aids to use as we tell the story twenty years from now about the how the big buildings fell and . . . well, whatever happened next, which is as of yet unwritten.

Amidst shelves and shelves of tiny Empire State figurines and Statue of Liberty plates, bells and shot glasses, one lone ceramic set of the WTC was left: a gray, muted figurine with very little detail, appropriately understated enough to be the solemn keepsake it will now become. On one side, the base said "New York"; on the other, "Twin Towers." These words speak a whole new language today.

In a somber stupor I started my trek back uptown to my apartment. Barely twenty-four hours later I was making the same curve around Columbus Circle—in the opposite direction—and I saw a burgundy truck pulling bales of something out the back doors. They just kept coming by the ton. I couldn't quite believe it—it was the *New York Times*. Tons of them, spilling out everywhere. As fast as they would pull a bale out and clip the plastic band, handfuls would disappear behind other people's dollars. No one was even counting. *Here's my money. I don't care what you charge.* I bought five of them. And I went home and sat on my floor as I turned from page one to twenty-five and then started back at one again. A few pages later, I made a phone call. "Have you read this? What an awful picture; I can't read any more"—then back to page one.

None of this was "cool" or fun. The T-shirts were not bought as souvenirs. Instead, it was like rushing home after the news of someone's death to see if you still had that letter they'd written, that movie stub from last summer, that very last Christmas card. The reason this article turned into reminiscence is to fully explain what I began in the beginning. New York has been further distracted while the world started healing. We lost a few days of work. We tried to think economically, globally, politically, personally, but all we could do was watch the smoke billowing and wonder if, when it clears, they'll be back, standing there, right where they belong.

Today, we finally started to try to catch up. We have finally started talking about our sons and daughters enlisting. Finally started doing things like, oh, laundry. For the first time today I saw kids from a school selling memorial pins to raise money for the FDNY. The rest of the country has been doing this since day one. (I know I cannot even begin to understand where the rescue workers—not only in New York, but at all of Tuesday's locations of destruction—fall in the recovery line. We must understand that none of us can fully understand.)

But in NYC, half of us have been wandering downtown block by block, as the barricades have been pushed further back, to see if it really happened, to feel it for ourselves. The other half of us have been cook-

ing hot meals for rescue workers, driving caravans of pet owners by police escort past Canal Street, shuddering at the Empire State Building.
Some of us have been trying out new office spaces, singing hymns at
the Armory while waiting for news of the missing or attending funerals.
We've ended up a very long beat behind the pulse of America. But
we're starting on the make-up assignments now.

Be patient with us. We still know north from south, but we tear up
when we use the sun to find our way, instead of its two favorite vanity
mirrors.

I'm even watching the Presidential Address. In my apartment
alone I applauded the President and the moment in time. I will continue to do so, but I will do it with my respect, my prayers, my ambition, my humble attempt at service and selflessness. I will rewrite
the definition of "American" in my own life.

If we do it together, this country can be the definition of God's love
for man. If it's not too much to hope, perhaps the whole world will
clearly see and understand this love, this strength of character, this
blessed assurance. Perhaps one day soon, they will look up to check the
color of the sky on a free and hopeful evening and exclaim, "My goodness, this really is God's world, just as He said. He really does love us after all."

Part 5

I Love New York

"New York is a beautiful country."

—A favorite saying among the employees of Windows on the World, the restaurant at the top of Tower One at the World Trade Center

Before September 2001, I was not your quintessential New Yorker. Though a NYC resident of ten years, I have a small-town heart, a love for the land, a need for a far-stretching sky. Now, I will in large part be a New Yorker 'til I die.

I would proudly associate myself with the character and spirit that erupted from these city streets. People came from all over the world with the same commitment to heroism, service and love. But in a moment of unprecedented national and local crisis, there was an unusual sentiment. Suddenly, everybody loves New York.

It's that New York is "The Crossroads of the World." It's the diversity of the people, and that we choose to be together. Just like America in general, we may have our faults and fights, but we are a family.

I won't candy-coat it: New York is not altogether a decent, upstanding, moral place. It's a city and it can be the worst of the worst.

But it's also the best of the best. Someone said once, "Where there are the strongest of demons, there are also the greatest of angels." We met a few from both camps on September 11, but it seems since then, all I've seen are the angels.

New York has always been a celebration of extremes and excellence. It seems the one thing we sometimes fell short of was the humility. We have found it. We are not invincible. We are vulnerable. We are not perfect, but we strive. We are not always loving, but shown our ways, most of us would take a step back and extend a hand to our unfamiliar brother and learn to walk the same mile together.

And moreover, people love New York because New York is hurting. It is the tremendous tendency of the American spirit to love those who are hurting, lift up those who have fallen and heal those who are brokenhearted.

The whole world was hit, not just Manhattan, but the unique experience of this city and the role its residents played throughout the days of September and beyond, have struck a fascinating chord of love, gratitude and shared sorrow. I love New York because the firefighters still put on the uniforms that are almost too hard to look at. I love New York because people who have lost loved ones go back out into the street to minister, to help, to work or to pray for someone else's loss. I love New York because 8 million very different people are living in the same house, learning to live together; because the streets of New York have found kindness—very different from simple hospitality; because the people of this tragedy are trying so hard, and they should be rewarded with unconditional love.

Autumn in the City is drawing to a close, the lights are shining brightly, from Broadway's grand gusto to go on with the show to the new evergreen in Rockefeller Center—just arrived for the holidays. I will be there on Wednesday, November 28 for the lighting of the tree, to see the twinkling lights catch their Christmas fire. It will be the most extraordinary lighting ceremony Rockefeller Center has ever hosted. Much more than a Christmas tree, we will gather boldly and joyfully at the "uptown-ground zero" where the first trace of anthrax was found, and we will shine. Our hope, our faith, our "joy in all circumstances" (Philippians 4:11, author paraphrase) and our determination to carry on for the lives lost will shine from the heart of Manhattan. The tree we all came to see just might get lost within the brilliance of the hearts surrounding it. And in that collective light we will sing, "O, Holy Night, the stars are brightly shining . . ."

For marvels such as this, I absolutely love New York.

"We're Going to New York"

Dave Odgers is from my hometown of Sacramento, California. He actually lives in the same small, rural area of Sacramento where my parents live—Antelope—where he is a firefighter and a member of the Urban Search and Rescue Team.

With all the stories pouring in from around the country of rescue workers and helpers doing the their part, this one coming from my own hometown reminded me how closely we are all connected.

My mother, Diane Bartlett, who is also an author, had a chance to interview him when he returned to Antelope. She writes of this "silent hero" and the others who traveled 3,000 miles to Ground Zero with him:

> We watched as their lives were endangered beyond the pale along with the rest of the victims of that day. We watched as they banded together from across the nation to clean up the devastating aftermath. As we return to work and what's left of normalcy, they remain on the scene—shocked, appalled—but diligent to the task that few of us could tolerate or stomach.
>
> Dave Odgers is one of our Antelope neighbors. He and his wife Mary Ellen are local natives, high school sweethearts, friends since kindergarten, who met, grew up, married, had children and settled right here at home. But as a career firefighter/engineer with Sacramento Metropolitan Fire Department's Station 21,

Odgers occasionally gets called away to help others in distress—sometimes far from home; sometimes to Oklahoma . . . sometimes to New York City.

He has been part of the Urban Search and Rescue Team since 1993 and has witnessed repeated scenes of disaster. But Odgers admits that nothing compares to the disaster he was to witness on September 11th.

When asked to explain how he, and others, find the character and strength for such a mission, Odgers simply explains, "We're Americans."

Dave was at work when his wife called the station and told him to turn on the television. He watched the first plane veer into the building but had to leave for a class he was scheduled to teach across the street. Crossing that street was as little time as it took for word to come in officially.

"Go home and pack your bags. We're going to New York."

He talked to his kids as he packed—he'd pulled them out of school. A short six hours later he was in a C5A aircraft departing from Travis Air Force Base in Fairfield, California. Thinking of the men on that plane tugged just a little extra on my heartstrings . . . Travis AFB is where I was born.

In the air, they were reviewing their field guides, preparing, talking, when the pilot made a surreal announcement.

"We are, right now, the only plane in the United States airspace."

Technically, they were one of five, but the other four were the USAF F16's that surrounded them. That was the pilot's second otherworldly announcement.

"Right now, we have a four-fighter escort. We are the first civilian personnel ever escorted over the United States."

When they arrived at a base in New Jersey it was 5 a.m. on the 12th of September. They had to be ready to go by 6.

Coming from the New Jersey side, they actually entered Manhattan from the east, coming across the Manhattan Bridge. Now, for anyone who doesn't know the lay of the land around here, let me explain the oddity of this. From New Jersey there were several tunnels. At this time they were closed—even to rescue personnel.

They had to be bused down, southwest through New Jersey, across the Outerbridge Crossing into Staten Island, across the Varazzano-Narrows Bridge, up from Lower Brooklyn, almost to the border of Queens, before they could get in through the Manhattan Bridge. It was an unreal day when, for the most part, Manhattan was closed.

Among the rescue teams from all over the nation, he was in one of four teams sent from California. California has eight such teams, only four of which can leave at a given time. FEMA asked for all four.

On the first of his twelve-hour night shifts, he described the scene with haunting similarity to every other worker to whom I've spoken. "Where do we begin?" he said. "It's just so big."

Just like the cops from the West Side Highway had observed, he said everyone was pitching in, doing their thing. "We all think the others are crazy for doing the jobs they do—the cops couldn't imagine doing the firemen's jobs, the firemen don't want to work construction—but then when it comes to ourselves, well, we're just doing our jobs," he said, laughing. "We're all just doing the best we can with the talents God gave us."

And that's the only way he could even get started in a task of this size—just pick out a piece of the pile and do the best you can.

His job was to search the underground voids for people to rescue or at least recover. He searched in subway tunnels and deep, narrow holes. "You wouldn't think about the dangers until you crawled back out of the hole and looked back and thought, 'Wow.'"

Those pieces of the tower's wall we've all seen jutting from the ground are actually embedded about four stories deep.

He described wide craters six floors below the surface, with ten steel stories still towering above ground. "You'd look up at sixteen floors of total devastation and do a complete 360-degree turn. . . . Sad."

One thing they were beginning to notice: in the remains of one of the largest business complexes in the world, there were no desks or other office furniture. Small things had survived, such as papers and pictures, but everything else was just gone.

This realization, along with the repeated task of "marking" a body and moving on (bodies that were found under immovable beams and debris were marked until they could be retrieved later) would have taken its toll on him, were not for his faith. "I'm a firefighter, we're trained to get them out. It's sobering to have to leave someone behind and go on.

"But it's not on my shoulders to deal with. I just gave it to the Lord. You have to. It was a grim job, but we [the team from California] considered ourselves 'the lucky 64.' We got to go, we got to help.

"The Lord was over us—over the whole site—and I don't think anyone would deny that. We were protected, too. No major injuries. It made the difference. I can do my job because I don't have to worry. I know I'm not alone."

Before Dave and his crew headed back to the Golden State on the 20th, they were given a night out on the town. New York doesn't know how to stop being New York, no matter what has happened. So our brothers from across the country came to the very center of the island in Times Square to discover we were still making pizza, still blazing the lights and, in the midst of it, still drying tears and shaking hands.

With about fifty of them dressed in their "search and rescue" shirts and shorts, they drew a lot of attention and a lot of cheers. People applauded from their balconies, strangers stopped to say thank you. The driver of one of those oversized SUV/Limousines (a huge Ford Explorer stretched into a limo) that carry the tourists around for a price called them over and said, in a great New York accent that Dave couldn't help playing with, "Get in—I'll take yous around da downtown!"

"We were treated so well by the people of New York and I have to say 'Thank you.'"

It's a common sentiment nowadays. When they landed back at Travis the next day, there were "thank you" signs plastered everywhere all the way back to Antelope. "I tell you, every overpass from Fairfield to Sacramento, an hour-and-a-half drive, was packed with people waving and shouting; some had fire engines parked on the overpass with the firefighters in salute. Other engines would join us on the freeway and escort us through their town, lights and sirens blaring, celebrating. We didn't realize how much it meant to people. We had no idea.

"People felt good, they felt helped. They wanted someone to thank. . . . We were just a bunch of firemen, doing our job."

They all say the exact same thing—"Just doing our job." But thank you, Dave, and all the men from your team. Thank you as well to the ones from Minnesota, Iowa, Texas, Oregon, Arizona, Virginia. Thank you to all fifty states' worth of humble workers who came in to help and to "just do your job." Thank you to the families that loaned them for a while and trusted they'd be safe.

Thank you to the families of the rescue workers, firefighters and other personnel who got the call first, and who gave their lives "just doing their jobs." We don't know quite how to thank you because we know we can't even begin to understand. But we try. And we're here. We will try to be here for you, as a community, as the family you deserve.

And thank you, most of all, to God—from me, from all of us, for everything and for holding us now.

On Calm Waters

On Sunday, Billy Boyd can be found singing playful little songs with powerful messages—the fun and jumpy kind of music kids absolutely love, where they get to wave their arms around on the chorus and shake their toddler tails. It's a joyful sight to see grown-ups like Billy and his wife, Cathy, playing and dancing and singing, both with their guitars. And the kids adore them.

But Billy has a "day job," too. On the weekdays he works for Sodexho food and facilities management service on the 57th floor of Trade Tower One—or, at least, he did. He and the rest of the staff would arrive around 6 a.m. to get the day started.

He was at work on September 11 when he felt the plane hit the building; he thought it was a bomb. The noise, he explains, was like a hammer hitting the wall next to your ear. The building rocked back and forth, and things were falling off of shelves like a ship in stormy waters.

It wasn't difficult to find the correlation between Billy's comments and the description of Jesus calming the waves in the Bible. "He got up and rebuked the wind and the raging waters; the storm subsided, and all was calm. . . . They asked one another, 'Who is this? He commands even the winds and the water, and they obey him' " (Luke 8:24-25).

Billy mentioned more than once the lack of panic and the sense of calm—not only within himself, but in everyone else—that day. But it started with him alone and, confident in the Lord, he began to make decisions.

He stayed to clean up a little, putting things away and turning off the stoves and ovens. He didn't know when he'd be coming back, whether it would be later that day, the next day or later than that. But he assumed he would at some point be back. He abandoned his belongings and left in his chef's uniform. It didn't yet exist in anyone's mind that such a structure would not only crumble, but somehow, inexplicably, also disappear.

So he left, still wearing his big rubber chef's clogs. Everyone was caught in the middle of their day in "costumes" that didn't match a scene of war. We picture war in different backdrops, with different scenery and different people. But a chef's suit? There were people in business attire, police and firefighters, coffee vendors on the street. Something unspeakable had happened on Main Street, USA. Like something out of place at Sesame Street, these were just the people in the neighborhood.

Billy went up a couple flights to look for his boss, whose office was in an area that had a private stairwell. Like everyone else I've talked to, Billy described the scene in the stairwell as calm and helpful. "Many people thought it was a bomb. Those who had heard something about a plane thought maybe a small plane. And then there was another incredible sound—a shaking." No one in that stairway had any way of knowing then that their tower's twin had just come crumbling to the ground.

"We were spared from knowing," is how Billy put it. "If we had known anything—the terrorists, the other planes, the danger—there might have been panic and a stampede. There might have been paralyzing fear." But they were spared the knowing.

Calmness prevailed, "the peace . . . which passeth all understanding" (Philippians 4:7). The Holy Sprit walked down the stairs next to and within a thousand hearts whispering, *I am with you; all is well, even now; be still and know that I am God.* Even for those who didn't know Him, He was still there, with the same message: *Know. Be still and know.*

On the stairs, people were making room for the injured and their helpers to get down more quickly. It was a constant stream going down, except for a few very memorable faces going up. They were the firemen—young, old, sweating—carrying both gear and duty square on their shoulders in their last great marathon.

Billy Boyd tried to help; he offered to carry some of the equipment up the stairs to get them there faster. They told him to go—to get out of the building. One woman told him he could use her cell phone when they got out—the phones in the enclosed stairwell weren't working. They still had no idea what they were about to find on the ground level. "The bandstand was gone, the things you saw everyday," Billy began. "It was a different world already—a movie set, unreal."

The elevators were blown out; debris was falling from the ceiling throughout the courtyard. They were led downstairs into the mall, where they were met by an even more unreal environment—water flooding the floor; darkness; more water dripping from the ceiling.

And then they were out—but not out to safety, just out. "Don't look," they were told as they stumbled over debris and, for the first time, into the realization of the severity of what was happening. "Don't look up; just go."

Amazingly, Billy ran into the woman who had offered in the stairwell to let him use her cell phone; he called his wife Cathy. She had been on the phone with a friend who saw the building come down. "How can you be so calm?" the friend asked. Cathy and her husband Billy, miles away, were holding the hands of the same Savior together.

A few blocks up, Billy found a huge crowd on the street, watching. He ducked into One Chase Plaza, where he used to work, and went up to the 47th floor to find his old boss. He noticed others watching from a high embankment; when the second tower began to fall, the thousands on the street and on the balcony scattered. One man jumped off the balcony onto a hot-dog cart and broke his leg. A van came by to take him to triage. It was time to leave altogether, Billy decided. But by this time the elevators in this building had also been closed. He began to walk the stairs for the second time that day, another forty-seven flights.

Back on the street when he looked back over his shoulder, he said he was struck by the fact that he couldn't see the sun. It was the middle of a gorgeous day and the light in the sky was blackened. But the light of the Lord was shining more brightly than ever.

The stories rolled in: a Muslim man lifted to safety by a Hasidic Jewish man who stopped to read the Arabic prayer on the man's necklace medallion; two blind men guided by the seeing eye dog that belonged to only one of them—a dog that was trained never to hurry, but somehow knew there was urgency that day and ran them out of harm's way.

There was the man who opted to stay behind with an overweight man who had been overcome and couldn't make it down any further; his coworkers made it out to tell the story of their hero friend who stayed behind and gave his life just to "be" with someone who was stuck and frightened. There was the woman in the wheelchair carried down seventy-two flights. There were the dozens of burn victims who, under their own power, made it to ambulances waiting so many floors below—even though they were burned over eighty to ninety percent of their bodies.

There were four firefighters who assisted an elderly lady, which slowed them down just enough that, at a critical moment, they were caught in the only safe spot around. They put their lives in danger to help and were in turn given their life.

As Billy began to walk away from lower Manhattan, his heart was struck by the line of fire trucks, unable to go in any further, sitting perfectly still, quietly filling the street in rows, waiting. These mighty machines and willing heroes were not yet able to enter the scene of disaster. But God was there. "The LORD will fight for you; you need only to be still" (Exodus 14:14).

Billy mentioned Psalm 57 and as he did, I could hear in his voice his love for God. I could hear how he remembered, with fondness and gratitude, his Savior who was with him beneath the ashes: "Have mercy on me, O God, have mercy on me, for in you my soul takes refuge. I will take refuge in the shadow of your wings until the disaster has passed" (Psalm 57:1).

He walked with his friends—and with thousands of others in that unfortunate, modern-day Exodus—up to Calvary Baptist Church on 57th Street. Pastor David Epstein was waiting outside the door. He was ready; Christ was ready; Billy was ready.

"Be ready," is Billy's message. "It doesn't stop at inviting Christ into your life; it's about keeping Christ in your life. If you call out He will answer. He will comfort.

"Those who made it out, who were spared or guided away, we were not given 'a second chance at life.' It's not like a cat with nine lives. We get one chance. We get one life. Now, we go forward with it."

Eighteen
"Jesus to the Rescue"

With its front doors wide open, David Epstein's church has weathered the recent events with new stories, new family, new ties to the community and new praise. But one of the most endearing connections began shortly before September, when more than seventy children headed down the street to the firehouse.

The children of Calvary Baptist Church had a chance to meet the firemen in the church's neighborhood before it was too late. As part of that summer's Vacation Bible School, they went on a "field trip," one and all—Pastor Roy Roberts, the pastor of youth education, Sunday school teachers and more children in tow than you can easily count on a busy city street—to the firehouse, just one block up. The firemen of Company 23 not only met and talked with the kids, but they also took the whole group on a tour of their station house on 58th Street and 7th Avenue.

By extraordinary coincidence the theme and title of the Vacation Bible School they held that summer was "Jesus to the Rescue."

That was August. A month later, six of those favored firefighters—the heroes who shared their day with the children—were gone.

It's a difficult thing for the children to digest and endure. But love—*that* they understand—and they began immediately to "do something" for the men they'd just met and the families that each one left behind. They collected $400 to bring back to the firehouse and, of course, the staff and congregation were able to assist even more. When the firemen received these gifts from the children, they came to the church with tears and hugs.

131

It's not just the firemen who have newly come with tears and hugs to the front doors of Calvary. A Roman Catholic police officer came in to hug the pastor, to cry and lean on his "brothers in Christ."

A Jewish man came and said, "My synagogue is too far; may I come in and pray here?" The question didn't even need to be asked. All are welcome at Calvary; no one is turned away. Had I been there that day, had I been given the chance to talk to this man, I would have said, "My friend I have been at Calvary's altar myself to worship the God of Abraham, Isaac and Jacob—to place myself at the feet of *Ha Shem*. I know your Father, the One who created us both, and I love Him as my Lord. I would be honored to pray at your side."

The doors of the church have always been open to the entire community, but suddenly the community is coming in. We are acting less like church and state and more like family—on both sides.

The morning of the attacks, Senior Pastor David Epstein and his staff met briefly in his apartment above the church to "watch and pray"—to watch the news unfolding and to pray for God's grace to minister healing to others—before going downstairs to throw the doors open.

A few members of the Calvary family were the first to arrive. They told their stories, prayed and hugged. Their needs were met in any way possible—showers, prayer, money, clothes.

Sam Jimenez, Jr. was there. His father had been waiting to hear he arrived safely. He first got a call from his son at 8:55. "Dad, we've been hit, there's smoke in the building, turn on your television." Sam Sr. was left, like the rest of the world, watching and waiting until 11 a.m., when his son called again from a Police Command Station. He was fine, and on his way to Calvary Baptist Church, where he arrived covered, like his fellow refugees, in dust and ashes. His pastor met him there and gave him a clean shirt to wear.

David Epstein shares a bit of what he is experiencing now as a midtown pastor, along with his hopes and prayers for our times, in the following letter:

A Time for Hope

It looked like a scene from Beirut or Kabul: a long line of refugees, dusty, frightened, in shock, semi-lifeless. But it was not the Middle East—it was 57th street in New York City, as the "refugees" escaped north, miles from Ground Zero. Some were members of our own congregation, who had escaped the Twin Towers from as high up as the 87th floor. And we, along with hundreds of churches, had the privilege of offering spiritual, emotional and physical help—the love of God.

We are at war! A day of evil, September 11, 2001, has provoked our nation to respond with Operation Enduring Freedom to punish Osama bin Laden and destroy state-supported terrorism. Our enemies hate us for our freedom, our faith and our friends (especially Israel). And by attacking the World Trade Center and the Pentagon, two strong symbols of our national power and prestige, the terrorists hope to bring down our nation and our way of life. But what they don't understand is that America, for all our financial, scientific, political and military power, is ultimately built upon our faith in the living God, the God of Abraham, Isaac and Jacob; God the Father, Son and Holy Spirit. Therefore, "We hold these truths to be self-evident, that all men are created equal, that they are endowed by their Creator with certain inalienable rights . . . among these are life, liberty and the pursuit of happiness." To topple our nation, our enemies must destroy our faith and trust in God—a daunting task!

As God's people, our duty is to wage spiritual warfare, even as our brave soldiers fight physically in Afghanistan. God promises that " . . . if my people, who are called by my name, will humble themselves and pray and seek my face and turn from their wicked ways, then will I hear from heaven and will forgive their sin and will heal their land" (2 Chronicles 7:14).

In the days and weeks following the terror of 9-11, as we opened the church for prayer and comfort, we experienced a number of divine encounters. On one memorable day, right after the first anthrax scare in NYC, a young professional woman entered the sanctuary right off 57th Street. She was focused and excited as she exclaimed to me and to an assistant pastor, "Please help me to find God today. I can't go home before I know God." We then had the joy of sharing God's love for her in Jesus Christ. She bowed her head and prayed, acknowledging her sin and asking God's forgiveness, expressing the desire to give her life to God and to follow Jesus Christ. She left joyful, confident and enthusiastic about her new life in Christ—just one more living example of how God produces beauty from ashes.

We live in an unprecedented time of spiritual opportunity. God is drawing many hearts to Himself in this time of loss, anger, fear and uncertainty, because God's love and power are greater than the evil around us. In this battle for the minds and souls of men and women, may we be found faithful, knowing that God has called us to His Kingdom "for such a time as this" (Esther 4:14).

—Pastor David Epstein,
Calvary Baptist Church, NYC

Brilliant Lights
on the Bowery

On Manhattan's Lower East Side, there's a mission that's been rebuilding souls and mending broken lives for 121 years. On September 11th, the people of this mission were prepared, willing and able to turn around and serve the community in which they had been given a second chance.

Ed Morgan, president of The Bowery Mission, was far uptown at the United Nations when the planes hit and the towers fell. The story he tells is a poignant one that, surprisingly, the press didn't comment on. He describes an island of untouched peace and prayer while, unbeknownst to a unique gathering of people, the city literally toppled around them.

Miroslav Volf from Yale Divinity School was the primary speaker at the U.N. that day. This dynamic theologian and native of Croatia was, more appropriately than he could have known, speaking on Reconciliation Between the Nations. He must have begun, by calculations, almost exactly as the first plane hit the first tower. The General Assembly had gathered for the Annual Joint Ministries International Prayer Breakfast.

It wasn't that the U.N. didn't find out immediately. In fact, unknown to those at the breakfast, the facilities were being quietly evacuated. Somehow, no one informed or interrupted the ecumenical gathering in the General Assembly. During the entire time, no one came in, no one was notified, no one knew. At one point, an ambassador's cell phone rang. He reached in his pocket and turned it off. He quieted the world. They didn't know that outside, there was smoke billowing into the sky, that 5,000 lives had been lost, that the

135

world was about to be very different. They remained gathered to pray, to listen and to hope for reconciliation.

It was about ten minutes before 10 when Ed Morgan finally left the quiet, peaceful meeting and came out into the chaos. A cab driver pointed down the street drawing their attention to the smoke plugging the end of the horizon. Ed's first thought was, *I ought to be at the Bowery*. So he headed south.

He found a cab, not yet realizing that this was a miracle in itself; the situation was spelled out for him over the cab radio. With every passing block the scene grew more and more dim—literally—as smoke clogged the sun from the sky and the people who had come north were covered in dust.

But in the darkness of lower Manhattan, one of many brilliant lights were shining. Just as brightly as every hand that reached out to help another that day, there was The Bowery Mission, already set up out on the street with tables, people, food, towels—and the masses kept coming. There was a sign that read:

How Can We Help?
food, water, bathrooms, telephones

Mr. Morgan's son was down in the financial district, on Water Street. He hoped that his son was fine. Then he got to work.

"The morning of the attack," he wrote, "we served more than 3,000 people, some of them covered with dust and debris. We provided everything from cold water to directions to the blood banks to a public TV in the fellowship hall. We gave away over 600 Bibles. We counseled with dozens. Our program men all began serving drinks voluntarily. It was good to see these men, who have been through so much in their lives, doing this for others.

"I've been so proud of the men at our mission—many of them fighting addictions and other troubles—pulling together to help the many frightened victims that came down the street. These men, who have often been ignored by the community, were the very people helping the community in its hour of crisis. That's what this mission is about—not only helping to feed and shelter, but also helping to build character in these men, so they can give back to the community."

"He Was a Bridge"

Lord, take me where You want me to go.
Let me meet who You want me to meet.
Tell me what You want me to say,
And keep me out of Your way.

—Father Mychal Judge, OFM

On September 11th, Father Mychal Judge died doing his job as chaplain to the New York City Fire Department. He doffed his helmet to administer last rites to a fallen firefighter when he was struck by falling debris.

They recovered him from beneath a felled fire engine and carried him to St. Peter's Church on Barclay Street. Six of his brothers acted as his first pallbearers, covering him with a white cloth and his prayer stole, then placing his helmet and chaplain's badge on his chest.

I talked to so many different people who knew Father Judge. They all had different relationships to the Franciscan priest, but they all described the exact same man. His character must have been tried and true.

The firemen closest to him weren't ready yet to talk. I didn't expect them to be. A few of his brothers at the monastery on 31st Street in the middle of Manhattan spoke wonderfully of him, sharing endearing quirks. One man started to recall, "I would go to see him in his room and he'd be throwing away a few pieces of paper saying, 'You've got to get rid of things, shouldn't hold on to everything.' Then when we went to his room weeks after his passing, we found stacks of papers in his closet. Turns out he kept it all."

137

When I asked this very kind gentleman a few more personal questions about Father Mike, as he was known, his eyes became red and he became silent. He wasn't ready either, just like the firemen in the station directly across the street from the monastery. "I thought I was getting past this, you caught me off guard." He and Father Mike had been friends for about half a century. I patted the back of his hand and I let him be. He had already told me the entire story in the tears building up in his eyes.

There were other voices to tell the rest. Steven McDonald is a New York City police officer who, along with his wife and son, was very close to Father Judge. They had worked and traveled together and been through quite a bit side by side. After calling Father Judge his best friend, Officer McDonald summed it up in a single sentence: "He was my idea of what a priest should be, and above all, he was an example of Jesus Christ."

I also talked to Father Michael Duffy from Philadelphia, who had worked very closely with Father Judge in the past. "He had no earthly airs," Father Duffy said, as he began to paint his picture of Father Judge. "He was just a human being. He was an image of peace and caring. He was a bridge.

"He was never preachy, but would gently bring God into every conversation, even in difficult situations. God *is* in every situation, and Father Mike would be sure to acknowledge Him and bring Him into focus, no matter who he was talking to—as simple as, God is with you. He was very calming and encouraging. He always uplifted people; that's why people liked him so much. When he was talking to you, you felt like you were the only person on the face of the earth. They responded to his love and to God's.

"No matter what it was, he was very forgiving and affirming. He would tell them, 'The grace of God is here, don't worry about it.'

"Some of the firemen used to say, when there was a particularly chaotic situation—a bad fire, heavy circumstances—they'd look over and see Father Mike and they'd know it was going to be OK."

That's our charge now, you know. We all have to be Father Mike's right now, or more realistically, what he was: the hand and heart and image of Christ. We all have to be the light that someone can look to and say, no matter what's going on, that it's all going to be OK.

Of all the memorial services being held even still as I write this, Father Judge's was the first and it was marked so on his certificate of death. It said simply, "1." Many commented that this was a significant element. He was the first one. "He went ahead to welcome the rest. He's there to welcome them."

Father Duffy put it in these words: "He's going to greet them with a big Irish smile. He's going to take them by the hand and say, 'Welcome! Let me take you to our Father.' "

It's a wonderful sentiment, but the most important component was that he did the same in life. He did it in his corner of the world and in his job with the FDNY. It's something we can all do in our own particular place, job and family. Its not just a comment to be saved for the "pearly gates." It matters even more in life to say to all, "Welcome! Let me take you to our Father."

American Trenches

Author's Note: I tried to keep the accounts in this book as free as possible from unnecessary details. But the whole story cannot be told without at least once considering the difficult facts of what the workers at Ground Zero encountered. Only then can we really appreciate what they have done.

It's not a task that can be ignored; someone has to do it. They were there and they were willing. For their sake and ours, the hard part has to be told. So I've included, in its entirety, a story by a local man, Steven Connolly. It's told in his own words, from down in the trenches.

I went into what they're calling Ground Zero at the World Trade Center on Friday morning, September 14, with my brother Paddy, who is retired from the FDNY and his son, Brendan, a Wall Street equities trader. We weren't sure what we would be able to do, but we were there to do whatever it is they needed.

You need me to get you socks, I'll get you socks; you need this box moved to there, I'll move it. I know you probably feel the same way and would do the same thing if given the opportunity. But the truth of the matter is that we wanted to be out among the rubble, assisting the firemen.

The scene was just unbelievable. There are no words to describe it. It was pouring rain, smoke all over the place. The smell of burning steel and asbestos was thick and got in your lungs and stayed there. There were literally thousands of people, from volunteers making sandwiches, handing out socks, hardhats, goggles, dust masks, rain gear—all sorts of stuff—to military, police, firemen, FBI and countless other agencies.

Anyone who knows me knows I love NYC as much as anything. I couldn't take it anymore just to watch on TV. Even though I'm not a

141

fireman, I come from generations of NYC firemen and policemen, including my father, who served as both a New York City police officer and then as a firefighter. Back in 1964, my father was pronounced dead at the scene of a fire in a building collapse, two blocks from where the World Trade Center would eventually be built. The news even identified him as dying at the scene. Fortunately for my family, the Lord allowed doctors to bring my father back and to this day he is a strong, healthy man who just celebrated his eightieth birthday.

Because of that background and having lost some friends in this tragedy, needless to say we really wanted to be out helping dig people out. My attitude was that if you're going to let a firemen from Des Moines get in there, you have to let me in there. It's my backyard.

They were only allowing firemen, some police, ironworkers and steamfitters out on the scene. I ran into some friends who are steamfitters and told them we were available to help in any way. My brother Paddy relieved some firemen at one of the rigs providing water to the fire. Brendan and I went with the steamfitters.

In order to get out to the rubble we had to pass through additional security points around the World Financial Center. The World Financial Center is only about twelve to fifteen years old and was one of the most majestic building complexes in NYC. If you've been down there or ever had lunch on the Hudson River waterfront at Moran's, you know what I'm talking about. The beautiful atrium, with incredible open space, palm trees and balcony, is now covered with inches of soot, broken glass, concrete dust, papers and office supplies.

We walked through the main entrance and eventually made our way out one of the side entrances to the job site itself. Not being trained emergency personnel, and never having been on a major construction site, Brendan and I really had no business being there. A major construction site in itself is a very dangerous place. The scene of a fire is always a dangerous place. This happened to be a major *destruction* site of two of the largest buildings in the world, with constant and numerous fire sources and a level of uncertainty about other massive surrounding buildings. It was very unsafe.

Walking through what now looks like a decades-old, vacant build-ing, we climbed down a spiral staircase to a small lobby with all its windows blown out, overlooking the heart of Ground Zero. It was an amazing site. You've seen all the images by now. But whatever you think it's like, multiply it by a thousand and then you might be close.

Our initial plan was to make our way out to the rubble and start handing buckets back and forth, but the first fifteen minutes we were there made me think that we might be in over our heads and not able to provide any real assistance.

I have been in some different circumstances in my life that have been rather surreal for me. I was in the Killing Fields in Cambodia many years ago. I was in Moscow in Red Square amidst the barri-cades during the coup in which Mikhail Gorbachev was removed from power. As I walked around Moscow those few days I didn't re-ally know what to think. More or less I felt like I was on a movie set. This really couldn't be happening. I returned from Russia a few months later that year and didn't get to see what was broadcast on CNN until then. What a small TV screen captures is not the same.

We've all watched the documentaries and fund-raisers for starv-ing children in Africa. They are difficult images to watch, but I've been in Africa and I've seen firsthand what goes on for those people. I can't even begin to describe the difference between what is reality and what we see on our TV.

There are a few other such scenarios I've experienced, but suffice it to say that the scene at Ground Zero is as unbelievable a site as you could possibly imagine.

As we stood in the lobby waiting to be deployed by a battalion chief onto the site, what was left of the glass was falling or hanging precariously. We needed to load up about a dozen five-foot-tall can-isters of acetylene and oxygen. When I heard the word acetylene and saw the falling glass, it was my first clue that I really didn't know what I was doing there, but I hoped I could help.

In order to get to the acetylene we had to move back out of the building a different way. As we turned the corner out of the lobby we entered a hallway that was absolutely pitch black, smoky and filled with about six inches of water. This was the second time I thought that maybe this was better left for the guys who knew what they were doing.

We finally made our way through a maze of hallways and got to the canisters. We loaded them up and headed back through the hallways. Guys were tripping over fire hoses submerged below the standing water. After we unloaded we brought the dollies back outside. As I started back in, my nephew said, "Don't you think we're a little out of our league right now?" I said, "Maybe, but let's go back and, if we are, we'll head out and help some other way."

That was all he needed. We headed back, not sure what we could do. When we found our way back to the lobby, we heard them say, "Grab a bucket." Brendan and I looked at each other and smiled, because we figured we could handle that. Or so we thought.

I grabbed a bucket and ducked down to step out a window and join a bucket brigade. As soon as I got through and straightened myself up, a body bag was shoved into my gut with a guy yelling, "Let's go; get this guy inside." So I dropped the bucket, grabbed the end of the Stokes basket and quickly brought it back inside.

The smell was unlike anything I had ever experienced. It completely overpowered the odor of smoke and burning steel. But I figured I had made it this far and these guys need help, so when we had completed the transport, I went back out again and made my way to a bucket brigade.

Even now, this was still an incredibly dangerous place. I can't begin to imagine what it must have been like the first two days for these guys. You have to climb a few stories over twisted steel I-beams that are wet, muddy and at all sorts of angles with spaces between them that pose their own risks for current workers needing to be rescued. One misstep and you may fall six to ten feet or more and need to be rescued yourself. Guys are falling frequently.

Workers had started at the perimeter and worked their way hundreds of yards in to the center of the towers. When the towers were built, they stretched hundreds of feet below the surface. This is where sub-basements, parking garages, stores, train stations, vaults, boilers and the like were located. During the collapse, a lot of the material piled up on the streets while the weight of the material that fell straight down pulverized itself. Consequently, they have to climb up over debris for a few stories in order to climb down a bunch of stories to cover the whole area.

There are crushed fire trucks, police cars, emergency vehicles, ambulances and cars scattered all over the place under the steel girders. Many times, we were standing on these rigs passing stuff back and forth.

Out on the line it was literally nonstop passing of debris one way and empty buckets the other way. They are basically taking this massive scene of rubble out in two-foot sections, or ten-gallon bucket loads, carefully identifying any body parts. These lines stretched for hundreds of yards from the perimeter to where the front line was. You started at the base and moved your way up the line as those in the front got relief, until you made it to the front yourself. Brendan and I were working on one line and there must have been five others that we could see and still more that we could not.

What I didn't think about, but obviously makes sense, was that you're not just passing debris back and forth; you're passing supplies. Since they are attacking this yard by yard and they can't get their gear out there any other way, we had to supply it manually. You'd hear a call down the line: we need twenty-foot ladders. Ten minutes later, half a dozen ladders would go up the line while debris was still coming down. We need acetylene, and 150 lb. canisters would go up the line. We need water, and dozens of cases of Poland Spring and Gatorade would go up the line. We need saws. . . . We need masks. . . . We need gloves. . . . We need fire extinguishers. . . . We need oxygen. . . . We need torches. . . . We need bolt cutters. . . . We need gasoline.

What you didn't want to hear, but it's why we were there, was, We need body bags, or We need Stokes. I never knew the name for the baskets that we've all seen on rescue missions when they strap someone in and lift them into a helicopter, but it's called a Stokes basket. I learned that more than I wanted to, hearing throughout the day, We need a Stokes. . . . We need two Stokes. And you knew that when two Stokes went up empty, then two would come back with body bags. This went on nonstop for the first five hours I was there.

After we had sent up a lot of equipment and moved a considerable amount of debris bit by bit, there was finally a momentary lull. There was not too much debris coming down the line. The sun finally peeked through. The President's helicopter flew overhead. F-18's were in the sky. It was a very, very bizarre, surreal feeling. On my line you could hear the saws working. With all the gear we had sent up, they must have dug themselves a little deeper and got into one of these voids we've all heard about.

Then we heard, We need all available Stokes! All available Stokes! Shortly after that the word came: Twenty-five Stokes.

There were a number of times throughout the day when you saw a Stokes at the front and you would hear, "Brother. Hats Off." And thousands of guys from every line would stop and take their hats off while a firefighter was sent down the line.

We spent about ten hours at the scene and seven hours on the line. My brother Paddy made it out to the front line and actually recovered a body down in one of the voids. Throughout the time I was there we passed down a lot of body parts, some full bodies. As they passed by, you would hear the whole range of emotions from the workers.

I just asked the Lord to have mercy on them.

I wish everyone in America could have the opportunity to stand on the rubble and assist in pulling a body out. I know everyone wants to help in that way. It didn't cause me any more anger or confusion or disbelief or bewilderment. It caused all of those things simultaneously and therefore it's too heavy to take in right now.

But one thing it absolutely did was transform my despair into hope. I no longer feel the way I did prior to going there, seeing what I've seen. I feel hopeful.

The volunteer effort has been amazing. To see people of all kinds pull together in this gruesome task strengthens you.

America, for all its faults, is still the best thing that God has allowed as far as societies go. Until He dictates that there will be peace—or until we invite Him to author peace—there will be no peace. With all its faults, no society in history has been a steward of peace and freedom like America. And for that, we cannot allow the forces of darkness to snuff out our shining city on the hill and we must realize that this battle is spiritual as well as physical.

I know that some of you have lost loved ones in this event and I bet all of you will be just a few persons removed from someone who perished. Many of you have family members who are spending countless hours on the scene risking their own lives as rescue workers.

I know you want to do something to help. I'm sure the Lord will show you a way if He hasn't already. Please know that I thought about each of you and stood there as an untrained civilian in your place wishing you could be there.

I know you are praying for those who lost loved ones. Please, also pray for the men and women who are on the scene because it's going to be very difficult to keep up the pace. Please pray in particular for the guys who are in the middle of it. The memories will not fade for them and I believe it's going to be very difficult for them to return to a normal life.

> God bless you,
> God bless America,
> God bless all freedom loving people.

—Stephen Connolly

From the Empire State
to the State of the Empire

From the window of my office, I could see the Empire State Building being evacuated. As it was drained of its people, it looked as if it was being drained of its blood, so pale, empty and afraid, having seen what happened to its twin brothers.

This wasn't September 11th. This was two weeks later.

Now the tallest building on the island of Manhattan, our skyline's new senior pride and joy, feelings about the building outside my window fluctuated from proud and grateful to just a bit wary. I peek at it every now and then; others come into my office, stand on the stool to peek too. Is it still there? What's going on? What are those ropes? Why are all the people on the street?

They were on the street because that Friday, one of several bomb scares was finally real enough to take some action and it was evacuated. We didn't wait for official word; we unofficially evacuated ourselves. Our building is just down the block and if it was more than just a false alarm, then it stood to reason that life was worth more than the last two hours of work on a Friday.

So there I was, standing on 34th Street, which was suddenly a ghost town after a few weeks of being the only major crosstown thoroughfare open at that time. It had been a constant convoy of sirens, a high-speed Fourth of July parade, and now it was empty—even roped off. I had my camera in my bag and I took a picture, if for no other reason than I'd learned my lesson that people and even places that we love can be gone the very next day. I took a picture just in case the Empire State Building decided to disappear that night.

Now, for the second time in September 2001, I found myself walking home up Fifth Avenue in the middle of the day. I lived on the West Side and the subways were on the West Side, but I couldn't bring myself to walk west. I just kept going north, staying my course on Fifth Avenue . . . again. I used it as an excuse to finally vent.

All right, Lord. I'm tired. I haven't slept. I don't have my family here to lean on, to talk to, to comfort and be comforted by. I'm tired and I can't even bring myself to let this out because of all the people who are missing someone right now.

I remembered a woman on the subway that morning. She was wearing a button with someone's picture on it. It looked like perhaps her mother or aunt. It looked just like every missing poster on every pole. A photo of someone smiling because the person taking the picture loves them. I wanted to ask her, "Your button—are you looking for her?" I started to several times. But old habits kicked in and I missed the chance to tell a stranger I really cared about the burden she carried pinned to her lapel. I told myself she'd be offended, or I'd run out of time with the train approaching my stop. Truth is, it probably would have made her day. She had a very familiar look of peace on her face. If I had said, "God's with you," she probably would have said, "I know," and been thankful for the understanding. But I held my tongue in a sleepy morning commute, and I missed my chance.

Now I remembered her. *How can I cry when she has to wear a button to get through her day? Would she understand if I wanted to mourn too? What would those who had hid under cars to escape from falling debris have to say about my grief over a bomb threat that probably wasn't even real?*

By 40th Street, I called a dear friend, Amy McConnell, who had been at the towers that day. I say at, not in, because she never made it further than the lobby. I thought she would understand the most. She worked for Guy Carpenter, Marsh & McLennan on the 51st floor of Tower Two. She was among the many who happened to be detoured by one thing or another that morning. She was on the ground floor talking to a colleague when the windows blew. She had been there, too, in 1993 and she knew enough this time to leave, immediately.

Her offices had relocated to the area I was walking through and I had just begun leaving her a message when I came upon a beautifully solemn crowd filling an otherwise public street. These days you never knew what could be going on around the corner in Manhattan. You even bent an ear when cabs pulled over to see if they had the radio on. In five minutes, the world can change. You wanted to be listening. All I knew, as I said good-bye to Amy's voice mail and closed my cell phone, was that whatever all those faces were doing over there together, looking in the same direction, I wanted to be a part of it. I wanted to look too.

I hadn't even realized I was at the steps of Saint Patrick's Cathedral. This is where most people had come running on September 11th. It took me until now to get to this town hall of hope and faith. I didn't really need to be here for my own sake, but I felt I should have come at some point in time to hold hands metaphorically with everyone else who had recently walked through the front doors for the same reason.

I couldn't go in just yet because, as I began to piece together, this crowd outside was an extension of the service being held inside. They were watching the simulcast on a screen the size of a truck, the spires of St. Patrick's reflecting in the black glass windows of the building behind it.

I found 51st Street closed to traffic—which seems to be a trend lately in this city. I had seen plenty of crowds this size filling these city streets before, but what struck me was the still position of every face in the crowd. I could see them all like portraits. They didn't move. From this distance you could convince yourself they didn't blink either. They watched a huge screen set up to broadcast what seemed to be a memorial service. Living here had already been one constant memorial service the last few weeks. The *New York Daily News* actually had a corner that featured information for "Today's Funerals." I didn't know if I could take the tears, but I realized I hadn't mourned yet. I hadn't attended an actual service. I hadn't gathered with my city to sing, to cry, to pray. So I took a place on a low stone wall and I became one of the still faces on 51st Street.

It was only then that I discovered which service I was attending, and it seemed like God had arranged the entire day—the evacuation, my route up Fifth Avenue—to get me here at exactly this time. Only a few minutes late, I had stumbled onto the service for the Marsh & McLennan Companies. I would later learn Amy McConnell was inside. I still had my cell phone in my hand from trying to call her. I turned it off and put it away and attended a service that was so much more than I expected it to be.

The mayor, with so many memorials to attend, found the time to be there and to say, "I believe they are in heaven." But the true image of changed time was apparent when the CEO of the Marsh & McLennan got up and spoke quite lovingly to his employees, reading from the Bible. He described an environment following the devastation of a people who actively cared for one another. There was a man who had come in, very understandably angry because he had been told, mistakenly, that his wife was safe and accounted for. She was not. When his anger had subsided, he actually came back and apologized. Still reeling from the discovery of his own loss, he found it within him to focus on the feelings of other people—people, by the way, who thought he had every right to be angry—and he came back to make things right with his brother.

There was another member of the company whose husband and two sons also worked in the towers. Of those three, her husband and one of her sons were lost. But one day after their memorial service, she and her son were there at a service of another Marsh & McLennan employee. Having been comforted themselves, they came now in comfort to others.

It is not only important that these things were done, but it is also important that they were noted as good and necessary—the way we should live and work at all times with one another. Like family.

And the CEO read to comfort them, "Now these three remain: faith, hope and love. But the greatest of these is love" (1 Corinthians 13:13).

There was another young woman who had lost her father. They both worked for Marsh & McLennan. But she found the courage to speak and to encourage others to be still in the trust of the Lord. Facing coworkers that she and her father had both shared, and now were only hers, she read an old hymn from the famous pulpit:

> Be still, my soul, the Lord is on thy side;
> Bear patiently the cross of grief or pain;
> Leave to thy God to order and provide;
> In every change, He faithful will remain.
>
> Be still, my soul, thy God doth undertake
> To guide the future as He has the past.
> Thy hope, thy confidence let nothing shake;
> All now mysterious shall be bright at last.
>
> Be still, my soul, when dearest friends depart,
> And all is darkened in the vale of tears,
> Then shalt thou better know His love, His heart,
> Who comes to soothe thy sorrow and thy fears.
>
> Be still, my soul, thy Jesus can repay
> From His own fullness all He takes away
> Be still, my soul, the Sun of life divine
> Through passing clouds shall but more brightly shine.

It was so fitting that these words—only excerpted here—fell on those outside under a bright new Manhattan sky where we were trying to comprehend the mercy we'd been shown, hidden within the devastation. It was coming clear now, just like the hymn said, beginning to shine more brightly with each cloud that passed away.

We stood in this sun and sang our hearts out to the sky. We shared our programs to read the words, but closed our eyes when the message hit home. We sang in the street with strangers, as life became our church. There was living praise in the streets.

As I looked out over the crowd I was struck by a very typical—but now very unusual—sight: a manhole with a construction pipe was sticking up from the middle of the street and steam billowed up through the crowd. Such a Manhattan sight. Just a part of the service now as we sang,

O God, our help in ages past, Our hope for years to come,
Our shelter from the stormy blast, And our eternal home!

Under the shadow of Thy throne Still may we dwell
        secure;
Sufficient is Thine arm alone, And our defense is sure.

There was one more hymn at this service. I have purposefully saved it for last. As I read the words from my neighbor's folded program I was so stricken by their exactness that I stopped singing. They spoke perfectly for this day, this moment, this portion of history as if they had been written in reflection and memorial to what we have just endured. And suddenly, even the concept of time seemed so much smaller as I realized anew that though thousands of years may pass, it is the same battle, and the same God.

These words, from so long ago, are made exactly for today. Read them with a careful heart and consider our state of current affairs. Read them with an open heart and consider God.

A mighty fortress is our God, A bulwark never failing;
Our helper He, amid the flood Of mortal ills prevailing:
For still our ancient foe Doth seek to work us woe;
His craft and power are great, And, armed with cruel hate,
On earth is not his equal.

Did we in our own strength confide, Our striving would
        be losing;
Were not the right Man on our side, The Man of God's
        own choosing:
Dost ask who that may be? Christ Jesus, it is He;
Lord Sabaoth, His name, From age to age the same,
And He must win the battle.

And though this world with devils filled, Should
        threaten to undo us,

We will not fear, for God hath willed His truth to
    triumph through us:
The Prince of Darkness grim—We tremble not for him;
His rage we can endure, For lo, his doom is sure,
One little word shall fell him.

That Word above all earthly powers, No thanks to them,
    abideth;
The Spirit and the gifts are ours Thro' Him who with
    us sideth:
Let goods and kindred go, This mortal life also;
The body they may kill: God's truth abideth still,
His kingdom is forever.

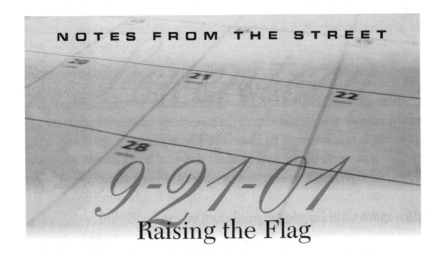

9-21-01

Raising the Flag

Today, New York City had a memorial service in the house that Ruth built. There were no Yankee baseball players, but there was everything else American. The mayor, the governor, Bette Midler singing "The Wind Beneath My Wings," shouting her tearful, overwhelmed thank-yous at the families of our lost servicemen. I recognized a woman from my church in the crowd and it suddenly became so personal and real. I was reminded these are not actors filling this stadium, not the politicians and the elite that filled the National Cathedral. These were the locals. This was Ruth from Calvary Baptist. These were wives holding their two sons against their chest as they sobbed for the man who no longer filled their home.

Another realization: there was something more missing from this crowd than those whose lives have been lost. There was another group that can usually be counted by the hundreds at memorial services such as these, but which has been noticeably absent today and recently: the brotherhood. When a serviceman dies from any brotherhood FDNY, NYPD, etc., it's tradition that all other members attend the funeral procession and service. A public procession, salutes of honor, the support for the family of hundreds in uniform that fight in the same capacity as the one that has been lost.

Now, these brothers are unavailable—unable to attend the funerals of the fallen because they're still working. They're still searching and re-covering. Though the chance of any rescue now has been called an im-possibility, they are still rescuing. And, I'm told, at Ground Zero, when a serviceman's remains are discovered, the rescue workers stand aside, if they're civilians, and grant the brothers of that department the re-spect of recovering the body themselves, complete with flag and salute.

Regarding the funeral services, there was a note on the table as I left work on Friday. It was a list of local funeral services, locations, times, directions, along with a plea for attendees. It was a call for anyone, strangers, civilians, community members, to attend the fu-nerals in a show of support in the absence of the units that would normally be in attendance. The list was long.

It seems when I sit down to send you these updates they often turn quite somber, as it's impossible not to do so after reflecting with such focus on the local scene. Even a simple trip to Burger King last night took us past the firehouse on 8th Avenue and 48th Street, where large groups have consistently gathered since all of this started, just as they have gathered outside almost every local firehouse in the city. All cliques: the media with their camera, talent and random interviewees; the well-dressed couples with coffee in hand; the guy on the bike from the village; those from the immediate neighborhood, for whom this firehouse carries even more attachment.

While we stood there and counted the pictured, remembered fire-men at 15, just for this house, a call apparently came in and the trucks began to file out, sirens blaring. As they did, the crowd applauded, al-most apologizing, and the trucks rang their bell, once each, in thanks. The chief's truck did the same, honking his horn. It dawned on me that we should be out here all the time, gathering spontaneously at fire-houses or police precincts to applaud the people who put their lives at risk every day to keep us safe. They are the same as American soldiers.

Here it was, still a day of aftermath, everyone focused on the trag-edy downtown and yet, like any normal day, the men from the 8th

Avenue firehouse had to climb in their trucks to do battle with a normal, everyday fire. If it's unrealistic to gather and applaud, how about sending a letter? Every so often, it might not be a bad idea to send a letter as part of a church, a youth group or a family, to say thank you to the veterans who work on the corner in our own neighborhoods.

But in the midst of the inescapable sobriety, there was a step taken today, an act of hope that took us another leap in the direction of healing. At the end of the memorial service at Yankee Stadium, Marc Antony and a substantial orchestra closed with a rendition of "America the Beautiful" that was intense, no matter how many times this week one has heard it. A subway rattled past on the elevated platform in the background, a sign of things in working order. And they began to raise the flags at the far end of the stadium, along with all the flags on the small poles atop the stadium wall. The crowd drew a collective breath as the star-spangled banners approached the half-mast position, and then, for the first time since September 11th, passed it.

The flags were raised in proud display of hope and strength and vigor all the way to the top. At Camp David, the President did the same. He stood in pledge of allegiance as the Camp David flag was brought to proud, high mast. Around the country, flags on government buildings, and elsewhere, did the same. And they flew there, untouched, unhurt, stronger than they were on September 10th. They flew for a stronger people; they stood for a unity that was more complete, a resolve that was renewed. Most of all, they flew for something we almost weren't allowed to say in public two weeks ago: they flew for one nation under God.

The flags are flying high again. Now let's get to work. Let purpose take its place. Let's not forget why they fell to half-mast, or why they fly high now. Let's get to work being the country we were intended to be, one family, one citizen at a time forming one great nation under God. Let your life be the flag you fly and fly it high.

Part 6

There Will Be Mercy Yet

Mercy came to America in so many different ways.

For many, mercy came in the form of obstruction, keeping the thousands from their intended route to work on September 11. Mercy was the peace of mind it took to walk down the stairs of a burning tower for hours, while making way for those in greater need. Mercy was the strength to break through a wall to get to freedom, or the strength to keep standing after twelve hours of hard labor and sights no human being should ever see. Mercy is even now in the homes that have been rocked with loss and devastation, providing the strength and will to get through and to turn what would be evil into good. "You intended to harm me, but God intended it for good to accomplish what is now being done, the saving of many lives" (Genesis 50:20).

And mercy is a gift to a nation that expends such an effort to remove God entirely, to push Him aggressively away. When the fire came, we called His name and found He was still there, still willing. Mercy was there.

It's still there now resting upon every man and woman who will but take it up. There would have been mercy for the terrorist pilots.

There would be mercy even for Osama Bin Laden, my brother still, if he handed his hatred to the Father. For the men of that regime left hiding in this country, there is a Father who loves you and all His children the same. No matter who you are, there is a God who knows you by name, calls you His treasure, says He takes His delight in you. There is an entirely new life even on this side of Glory. And there is mercy to the last moment, for the taking.

There is a story of a mother pleading with Napoleon for her son's life. "Please," she said, "please have mercy."

"Why should I have mercy?" Napoleon replied. "He certainly doesn't deserve it."

"No," the mother answered. "If he did, it wouldn't be mercy."

The Gift of Life

Mark Reamer knows what it's like, now, to be given the gift of life. It's something we all have and often take for granted. No matter how much we think we appreciate our families, thank God for another day, and, even when alone in life, are grateful for God's care and blessing, it's a whole different scale when you're faced with the possibility of losing it all, and yet are granted another day.

For many, this was the story at Ground Zero as they escaped unimaginable surroundings in miraculous ways. Mark escaped in a different way. He stayed home in Atlanta.

He was one of the thousands of "happened not to be there" stories—and no small number of those stories came from his company.

Mark works for Financial Fusion, a subsidiary of Sybase, the third largest financial technology company in the world. The miracles for Sybase stared early. Weeks before the attacks, the entire company moved their offices up a few blocks to Broad Street. They had been located on the 87th floor of 1WTC.

Mark works mostly out of his home in Atlanta, Georgia but travels to Manhattan, and elsewhere, frequently for work. He had just been up a week prior and was already packing his bags for another trip. There was a financial technology conference coming up. He was on the roster to attend and work certain portions of the convention—a couple days of product demos, passing out brochures, a sales meeting and (I'm sure) leisure time too, in the capital of the world. It was scheduled to begin at 8 a.m., September 11th on the 106th floor of Tower One at Windows on the World.

But he got a last-minute phone call.

His boss called him just one day prior and told him to cancel his trip. He protested a little. He had his plane reservation. There would be great networking opportunities, a good investment for the company. The answer was no, he had to stay. Besides, they would save the travel costs because, his boss explained, "I found someone to replace you."

Their names were Gaby Waisman and Clara Hernandez, two women who lived in New York, both of whom he knew, worked with and had just seen on his last trip to the city. They had helped him while he was in town, taking good care of him, calling a car to get him over to the U.S. Open and sharing the ride part of the way.

They were excited about the opportunity to attend this conference and talked eagerly about it, gathering all the information they would need from Mark. He told Gaby it would be pretty easy, walked her through the rigors of demonstrations and handing out pens. Clara bought a brand-new suit just for the occasion.

And it was done. A few phone calls, a couple business decisions on cutting travel costs and staying home to focus on end-quarter sales numbers. All that stuff that really doesn't matter in the scheme of life. It made all the difference on a day like Tuesday when Mark was home in Atlanta and the towers fell. Instead of a front-row seat from Windows on the World, he wasn't even in the theater. He watched from home behind a television screen. His wife had called to tell him to turn it on. He thought he was watching a replay of the horror, but it turned out to be the second plane going into the second tower.

Gaby and Clara, he knew, were on the 106th floor. They called one of his colleagues and said they had come down a little way but couldn't get past the 100th floor. The heat was too intense. It was the last anyone heard from them. They were both among the first couple hundred to be identified. They were in their early thirties.

As he unfolded his story, one line stuck in my head. I'm sure I missed a few of the details that followed, because I stayed on that one phrase, over and over. The choice of words his boss used to tell

him his business trip was off: "I found someone to replace you." The
words carried eternal weight. Not a flight, not a workweek, not a task.
Life.

He could have been on the 106th floor behind the wall that closed
the deal. He was home with his family—his wife, Jackie, to whom he's
been married for twelve years, and their three little boys, the youngest
one just four months new at the time the world around him changed.
So far we've changed for the better, though it took the worst. Let's keep
it that way. But Mark and his family hold on to one another today with
a greater awareness than yesterday. Perhaps with an even greater love.

There were others whose plans were redirected at the last minute.
Four men who were scheduled to be at the conference bright and
early got a similar call. It was 5 p.m. the day before, the last possible
minute of the business day, when Lehman Brothers called and requested a 9 a.m. meeting.

Could they? The conference started at 8 a.m. But for whatever
reason, the decision was made and they made the necessary calls to
say they wouldn't be able to make the conference until noon. Already, that meant an hour later that they would be expected to arrive
in the morning, and about seventy floors lower.

So, shortly before 9 a.m. the next day, they met one another in the
lobby, finishing their coffee and talking. That's where they were
standing when the windows blew out and the elevators exploded. In
a few more minutes they would have been in those elevators. Without the phone call, they would have been 1,000 feet higher in the
sky. But their feet were on a solid lobby floor and they walked away,
ran away, leaving their cars in the basement, with their laptops and
other belongings. It all became a part of the loss, but their lives were
not among what they left behind.

Another of Mark's colleagues started his day at the Newark airport, a
very common point in a frequent traveler's schedule. Nothing at all was
out of the ordinary; there were common sights and surroundings. He
stood at the ticket counter, waiting to head for San Francisco. The one
variable was a phone call—also not unusual on its own: a business-
man's cell phone ringing in the early hours at a busy East Coast hub.

But this call delivered a message that would pick him up and put him in a different place on one of the most impacting days in history.

"Don't get on the plane," his superior instructed him. "We need you here for a conference call."

He was told to transfer his ticket, drive over for the 9 a.m. call and go back to the airport for a later flight. He was in his car just across the Hudson River from Manhattan, listening to the radio; he could see the events, but he had no way of knowing at the time how directly involved he was. The newscasts continued, the horrible unfolding, and then, as they announced the flight that crashed in Pennsylvania, one familiar detail stood out as if someone had called him by name. It was his flight number. It was flight 93.

The distance between a New Jersey roadway and a cornfield in Shanksville, Pennsylvania was so much more than miles.

And of course there is the unanswerable question, why the others? Why were Gaby and Clara looking through the windows at the top of the world when the world suddenly collapsed? Only God knows, but in it He teaches us so much. He promises that they were not alone. Not only had He allowed them to be together, instead of just one person at the conference, but He promises He was there, calming, leading, lifting and most of all, guiding people to the literal home He's been building for them in heaven. Its not a figurative thing: ". . . we have a building from God, an eternal house in heaven not built by human hands" (2 Corinthians 5:1). He does not lock anyone out of His heaven, He invites them all: ". . . God our Savior, who wants all men to be saved and to come to a knowledge of the truth" (1 Timothy 2:3-4).

It is we who say yes and walk with Him, or say no. Thank you, but no. The two men who piloted those planes and banked left with intent had decidedly said no, or so we can assume from strong evidence. But another thing God makes clear: He doesn't shrug His shoulders and say, "Fine, whatever." For those men and, I'm sure, for many more, He wept. He ached. He reaches until there is no life left for which to reach.

I believe that day, some were able to grasp the hand of God.

I can't help wondering what greater, unearthly miracles there were there at the World Trade Center and the Pentagon and on four

American jetliners—for those who needed them most of all; for those next to whom God stood as they faced the inconceivable and then death. Did He speak to them audibly? Did they see His face? Did He say to them, "Be still and know that I am God"? Perhaps they felt nothing but joy and took His hand.

We have no way of asking them, but they are telling the story from all the corners of heaven as we speak. I pray the rejoicing there in the fold reaches our ears and that we hear it. I pray even more that we act.

The stories of miracles will begin to surface in greater volume over the years, and we will be more and more amazed by what God's hands did on earth that day. Maybe we'll even learn to see more clearly what His hands do on earth every day, and then go on to make sure others can see Him, too.

Twenty-Four

To Rise Again

On October 28th, 2001, the city of New York opened up the boundaries of Ground Zero for the first time and held a memorial service for the families of the victims. The cameras were there, but they were sensitive enough to explain that it was at the request of those who were unable to attend the services.

The cameras enabled all of us to see what we hadn't seen in the light of day for quite a while. It was a shock as, subconsciously, most of us expected it to look much better by now. If it's even possible, it looked worse.

The massive sadness of the vision took me to Calvary. It is a heartache that cannot be grasped. That innocence should be slain by evil.

I almost wanted to apologize to the families that I did not lose someone too, that I got through this without the same loss that they suffered.

It's October: the fires are still burning; the sprays of water from fire hoses are still flying higher than most surrounding buildings.

I watched some of the people at the service. Of all the indescribable countenances, a few truly gripped me for unusual reasons. A girl wrapped in a big coat and smiling a bit as her mom held her. She had braces. It showed me her youth, and how much she probably needed her father.

There was an older gentleman holding up a picture of a lost one. He was shaking a little as if he didn't know what to do with this loss, even now, a month later. Someone told him it was good—that he did a good job holding the picture up and he nodded with awkward relief as if he'd finally helped the man in the photo.

It was nearly too much to bear to watch the families and not be able to take away their pain.

But by the end of the service I realized this fact: There *is* an Easter Sunday in all of this. There *is* the possibility of rejoicing, the promise of hope. The Easter morning from 2,000 years ago is here now; it settles even upon Ground Zero. The joy of it is available.

Calvary is where the worst of sacrifice begat the single most powerful emancipation from darkness and pain—and the only victory, ever, over death. There was no separation between the destruction and the promise. Man destroyed the Son of God; God redeemed the sons of men—both together in one contained moment.

The scene at Ground Zero is so hard to behold. One can imagine, in the black spaces where offices and hallways used to be, those who were frightened that day; or in the empty space above the ground where two towers once stood, the even more gripping horror of those who were hurt or trapped, and those who are simply gone. And it's not fair. It's not endurable.

But there is a Messiah who could not be buried. There was no rescue for which to wait; He is our rescuer. So He moved the stone Himself and came to our side . . . and stayed. "And surely I am with you always, to the very end of the age" (Matthew 28:20).

There is the certainty of His resurrection to prove His triumph over death, destruction and evil; it means that we need not fear loss or vulnerability. We are not alone; we are not asked to shoulder this pain. He asks to hold it; He invites us to leave it at His empty grave.

God endured the pain of watching His Son be unjustly crucified—the utmost of innocence torn apart by those with other ideas of righteousness. But in that moment the temple curtain, twelve inches thick, tore from top to bottom, and through the name of Jesus, through the choice He made to stay silent on the cross and bear every sin, God's hands grasped ours.

There was a reason. It was because of evil. It was used for the ultimate good.

I am not comparing the loss of September 11th to the death of Christ as equal, but the two are interwoven. Just as the darkness of Calvary came with the promise of Life, so the darkness of our national despair. Unlike those who sat at the foot of the cross and wept bitterly, we can sit at the foot of the cross today and know that the light of Easter has already come. Like the morning when death was no more, now is our morning.

Those who watched Christ die would later walk with Him rejoicing. Now is our chance to walk with Him, and I tell you, if we do, rejoicing will come.

Twenty-Five

Her Call to Duty

Todd Beamer probably wouldn't have thought of himself as a hero, but he has been credited with helping to thwart the plans of the September 11 hijackers of United Flight 93, which crashed in a field in Pennsylvania. Knowing that death was imminent, Beamer, with the cooperative effort of several other passengers, selflessly stepped into harm's way to stop the plane from reaching its intended target—which, it is now known, was probably the U.S. Capitol Building.

This is Todd's story, as seen through the eyes of his wife, Lisa.

When I spoke to Lisa Beamer, she was in the car on the way to speak at the Women of Faith conference in Philadelphia. With the events of September 11th and the unique way her family was affected, Lisa Beamer has a new life to live. But she's the same person, in the hands of the same God as before, and has the courage to say that some things have even become stronger.

That's what she told me about her husband as well—that the man he was on the flight through Pennsylvania is not just a part of him that came out in a moment of crisis. It's who he was before, who he was every day and who he would have always been.

Lisa was still half-asleep that very early morning when Todd kissed her good-bye and headed to the Newark airport for an early flight.

He almost wasn't on that flight. I wish I could include his name in one of the many "happened not to be there" stories where a million last-minute miracles flew in to stop him from boarding. But though it may be difficult to grasp the logic of this, God had a greater plan.

The mercy was there in that the family was together the night before—one precious night. The mercy is there in the strength and understanding and peace that Lisa has now, not only to carry on and raise her children, but also to reach the world and encourage them toward the same peace, strength and understanding.

There are questions and pains of the heart, but she knows God, and as much as a human being can, she understands.

Todd and Lisa had just returned together the previous day from Florence, Italy, on a trip that Todd had earned through his performance at his job. He had considered flying straight through to the West Coast for his meeting the next day, but decided he'd rather be able to see the boys first; spending a night with them was worth the extra trip to the airport. He gave them their baths, said their prayers with them and tucked them into bed.

The next morning, Lisa was at home with her two little boys when news of the attacks came on the television. Everyone has their personal story of shock and reaction to that moment. Hers was no different. At the time, she didn't know what a pivotal character she would become in the event that changed a nation.

The reports continued. Flights out of Boston and Washington, DC had been hijacked; the Pentagon had been hit. Surely Todd was safe, but he would be stranded somewhere.

And then it came. A fourth plane, a United Airlines flight headed for San Francisco, but with a much more noble destination. It had crashed in a field in rural Pennsylvania, apparently saving the nation from a fourth disaster. Not only did it miss the White House, Air Force One, or any other imaginable target—it missed everything. With no control or direction it could have easily found an interstate, a home, a shopping mall. But it found only a field.

"I knew then," Lisa said. "A horrible, crushing feeling told me that Todd was on that plane."

She describes the network of support and the emotional battle of reaction that filled the immediately following days in a blur. Her parents helped with her children, her church family was there to help and to hold, friends everywhere she turned. But it was hard to sort the questions in such unusual circumstances. She wished she had at least a last word, one solid piece of information about what he had been facing. She knew just from who he was that he was solidly standing with the Lord on that plane and trusting in Him. But she had heard the reports of the phone calls from passengers and wondered if Todd had been trying to call.

It wasn't until a few days later when a small miracle came in—something Lisa thought she would never have. It was a call from a Verizon telephone operator with a message—from Todd.

The operator's name was also Lisa—Lisa Jefferson—and I can't help wondering if there was even more of a reason God put Todd in touch with this specific woman. I can just hear him praying, with his wife in his heart, "Please, Lord, help me get through to Lisa."

No, prayer wires do not get crossed. God didn't "accidentally" send him to the wrong Lisa. God is a God of immaculate detail. So I trust there was a purpose, some reason the two were meant to connect that morning. Perhaps it will be clear in the years to come.

Lisa Jefferson relayed Todd's message to his wife. "He was trying to get through to you," she explained, "but the phones were crazy."

Todd confirmed that a hijacking was underway. He stated that he and some of the other passengers had heard through other calls what was going on in the American skies that day and that they were going to take matters into their own hands before more malice could reach the ground.

He asked the operator to pray the Lord's Prayer with him. "His voice was strong," she recalled. "I could tell he was a man of his convictions."

In his words and actions, he was a testimony through the last moments of his life. If his voice was strong and calm, as the operator describes, it's a testimony also to the presence of Christ—his Friend, his Lord and Savior, so loved and so near in such a scene of ugliness. Todd was not alone; none of them were. But he was one of the ones who knew it, and knew the sound of His Father's voice before he ever set foot on that plane. Todd would be just fine.

This was not an assumption that that's how God works and therefore what Todd experienced. And neither is it just "faith." We know Todd was fine because he had a chance to say it.

"Mrs. Beamer," the operator said, "he wanted me to tell you this: that Jesus was with him up on that plane and that Jesus would be with you and the boys always."

The last thing the operator heard from Todd's now-familiar voice is the line we've all heard a million times by now. Lisa and her boys knew it as a part of their household language—a "Todd-ism." It was a common expression meant for lighter tasks, such as going off to church in the morning or getting the baths done at night: "Let's roll . . ."

Now it's the stuff of headlines and the words our country's President uses to close a speech. It's a call to duty, not just for what Todd and the others had to do on the plane, but for us, now. Just get it done. There are going to be tough tasks, bold expressions of faith and discipline. But fear or lack of determination will only invite unknown destruction. The threat is there; it will never be gone. Were there not a single terrorist on the earth, there is still evil. And there is still God. There are choices to be made.

Lisa set an example, one of many, on October 18 when she boarded a United Airlines flight from Newark to San Francisco to finish her husband's flight.

Just like Todd's sense of duty on Flight 93, and that there was no question about what it was in his (and the others') hands to do, Lisa has a task now, too. It would be a much more long-term one, but the Lord has been preparing her well, and she has accepted the responsibility.

"The one place the country's fear is coming from the most is the realization that we are not in control, the feeling of being out of control. I think this is a good realization, because it's true. I know we're not in control. But I know the One who is and I trust Him.

"There is the verse that says, 'If God is for us, who can be against us?' (Romans 8:31). This, not just applied as a country, or as a military presumption—though its promise is indeed for a nation, if its people turn to God—but as an individual. He is for me. He has "plans to prosper . . . and not to harm" (Jeremiah 29:11). And I know that's true. Though it may look ugly right know, I'm adjusting my earthy, human perspective through Him. I can see what He's doing and what He's purposing right now both for me and my family and for our country—and on the level of those He wants to know His promises.

"I'm living in these circumstances and trying to obey His will for my life and the path He's set before me now, and I know I'm going to come out with a stronger character and a stronger faith. I've already come out of it with a stronger love for God and a greater vision for what matters in eternity.

"Why are we here, going through all of this? There are two realities. One very human reality is that it is sad, that we grieve and mourn. But we also have a chance to look up and say the eternal perspective is even better. I've been challenged, and it is an incredible influence to examine your faith. You find all the little things it was so easy to get tangled up in before. Now they pale in comparison to the big picture, and we have a chance to grasp that, to prepare ourselves and to prepare others.

"The truth is, understanding our vulnerability, both as a nation and as individuals, is a good thing. Because in it we will also find there is One who is in control, and He is the One with all the power and all the love."

As word spread of the heroism on Flight 93, so also did the testimony of Todd Beamer's conviction that Jesus was his Lord and Savior. On a number of TV talk shows, Lisa reiterated time and again that her husband had absolute faith in Christ, and his life exemplified that to all he met.

When Russian TV reporters wanted to interview Lisa about her husband's Christianity, she invited them to Princeton Alliance Church in New Jersey. In the classroom where Todd taught Sunday school, the reporters saw a diagram on the whiteboard, depicting the chasm between man and God because of sin—and how Christ's death on the cross bridged the gap between them.

A Russian bureau chief, Eugene, commented that he had never seen anything like the bridge diagram and wanted to learn more. Eugene accepted Christ as His Savior that day. He returned to Russia to prepare a news broadcast about the Beamers that will be shown to millions of Russians. It will include the bridge diagram.

Our sovereign God has shown throughout history that He can use the most heartbreaking events to fulfill His purpose, bringing peace and healing to the lost and hurting. "You intended to harm me, but God intended it for good to accomplish what is now being done, the saving of many lives" (Genesis 50:20).

In the cloud of evil inflicted on the American people on September 11, this silver lining brings us renewed hope—hope in men who laid their lives down for others and in a loving God who longs for us to turn to Him in our time of need. For Lisa Beamer, that hope is her source of strength.

Passover

There's a little-known detail about the exact location where Flight 93 went down in Pennsylvania. I share this illustration with you, very respectful of the families of those on that plane.

I also don't claim to presume that this was indeed God's message. I take it as a point of interest and in the same spirit pass it on. But I do know that throughout the Bible, and throughout our lives, the God of Abraham is a God of detail and design. Everything that is from Him is consistent with His character and therefore has His voice and His way about it. I do find it just slightly more than coincidence, then, to find a direct correlation between Flight 93's granting us protection from further national suffering and the language and symbols of Passover.

With gratitude to God and, humbly, to every hero on board, we received the reports that Flight 93 had gone down on a hilltop in a small town outside Pittsburgh. The name of the town was Shanksville. The field that it hit ran up along a back road called Lambertsville Road.

Shanksville and Lambertsville.

The shank bone of the lamb is a prominent symbol in the Passover meal. The *Pasach* Lamb—or Passover Lamb—is a symbol of God's protection. It is eaten during the Passover meal, dating back to the first Passover in the Bible when God withheld His judgment from all the households who called for His shelter. The blood of the lamb on the doorposts served as a sign of immunity and protection. Today, even at Seders where the lamb is not eaten, the shank of the lamb is still present and acknowledged as a symbol of God's ultimate protection.

179

One pastor commented, "With this plane, He again allowed the full destruction to *pass over* the people of the United States. With Flight 93 pointing its nose toward Washington, who knows what building it could have destroyed and what effect that may have had on our national reaction and lasting morale? The Capitol? The White House? Symbols of freedom and democracy. I cannot imagine the devastating blow to this nation if the White House would have been destroyed. Substantially smaller than the Pentagon, there may well have been nothing left. And it's not the building—it's what the building symbolizes: all the history that has accumulated, the fabric of our nation."

I'm not one to play word games with the Lord's work, but I reiterate: He has often emphasized His resolution to provide by so perfectly authoring even the unnecessary details so as to assure us it is from His hands.

It's not so odd to find the deeper layers of God's design in our world today. Just as His promises aren't locked in the Bible, but are active in His world, the same meticulous, hidden details can be found in the Scriptures or in a field in Pennsylvania.

There's a very similar play on words in Genesis. It, too, is about protection, deliverance and a Lamb.

In Genesis, when God tells Abraham to offer his son as a sacrifice, Abraham obeys. He doesn't understand why God would ask such a thing, but in complete faith, he takes his beloved son Isaac—for whom he had prayed and waited so long—up to the exact spot on the mountain that God had instructed. When Isaac asked his father, "But where is the lamb for a burnt offering?" Abraham responded, "My son, God will provide himself a lamb . . ." (see 22:7-8, KJV).

It was on that same hilltop so many ages later that God indeed provided Himself as the greatest and final sacrifice. It is the place where Jesus, the Lamb of God, was crucified.

The story in Genesis goes on to put a fitting button on the correlation. God called to Abraham, saying, "Abraham! . . . Do not lay a hand on the boy. . . . Do not do anything to him. Now I know that you fear God, because you have not withheld from me your son, your only son" (22:11-12).

Abraham looked up and saw that God had provided a ram caught in the thicket. He named the place "Jehovah-Jireh," "The LORD Will Provide" (see 22:13-14).

He continues to promise, from Genesis, to Christ, to Shanksville, Pennsylvania and in so many other ways. What will it take for us to remember and to believe?

Indeed, "The LORD Will Provide."

Twenty-Seven

Do You See What I See?

It didn't matter who I was talking to—the stories were the same. They were lovingly individualized, full of different colors and intimate details, but underneath, all the stories were the same. Not surprising when the voice of one same God keeps ringing out.

Joe Smaha is part-time pastor, part-time member of a New Jersey HazMat team and part of the Fellowship of Christian Firefighters. He was on site at Ground Zero a few times, but his heart kept telling the story of God elsewhere, both on the 11th and ever since.

He told me about his nephew, Randy, who was among the many fortunate commuters running late for work that morning at Deloitte, Touche, Tohmatsu on the 52nd floor of one of the towers. Even more astounding was the fact that thirteen of the fifteen people that worked in that office were also "miraculously" late that morning.

A woman at Joe's church added her brother's name to the pile of "happened not to be there" stories. Gloria VanAntwerp's brother, Charlie Como, worked in the Twin Towers. His daughter's car wouldn't start so she called her dad and asked him to drive her to her doctor's appointment. He took the morning off to do her this favor.

Of Ground Zero, he recalls that the Salvation Army was ready within five hours—present on the streets at 1:30 p.m. after the attacks. He recalls groups of people dividing their time almost equally between working and praying. And he recalls ambulances everywhere, sitting quiet, not being used.

Brian L. Overby, a Marine stationed at New York's Fort Drum who was deployed to Ground Zero almost immediately, described the same presence out on the Hudson. The United States Naval Ship *Comfort*, a thousand-bed hospital ship, was empty, unneeded, unused. And yes, that is the ship's actual name!

These things began to take their toll. Brian was at the end of the second week of work at Ground Zero. It was a tough day; they had found an unusual number of bodies. He had watched one too many firemen saluted as their remains were pulled out with Stokes baskets, six other firefighters as willing but unwilling pallbearers, taken away in ambulances with a police escort. Just when he needed it most, his pastor called.

Focusing for a moment less on the devastation that had surrounded him all day, and more on the miracles, the smoke began to clear. He told the story of the woman and two rescuers who "rode the stairwell down" as one of the towers collapsed. They were somewhere around the thirteenth floor. A few more floors in either direction, and they would have been gone.

Then there were the two police officers who had been buried twice. They had finally decided to move their car when Tower Two collapsed. The place where they had been became a canyon.

Struck by the numbers of people spared and starting to focus again on the Spirit, Brian started to wonder how he could have missed the presence of God at Ground Zero—He was everywhere.

Before he returned to Fort Drum near Watertown, NY, He wrote a poem to read to his church once he got there. The title: "Where *Hasn't* God Been?"

Twenty-Eight

Elements of Mercy

"Where Was God on September 11?"
—From a contributor

He was trying to discourage anyone from taking certain flights. Those four flights together could hold over 1,000 passengers, yet there were only 266 total aboard. And for those 266, He was on their four commercial flights, giving terrified passengers the ability to stay calm.

Not one of the family members who was called by a loved one on one of the hijacked planes said that passengers sounded panicked in the background.

On one of the flights He was giving passengers the strength to overtake the hijackers and to lay down their lives for others.

He was busy creating obstacles for employees at the World Trade Center. After all, only around 20,000 were at the towers when the first jet hit. Since the buildings hold over 50,000 workers, this was a miracle in itself.

He was holding up two 110-story buildings so that two-thirds of the workers could get out. And the towers didn't topple sideways when they fell. This would have taken out thousands more in the surrounding streets and buildings. Lower Manhattan would have been as good as gone.

Although this is without a doubt the worst thing I have seen in my life, I can see God's miracles in every bit of it.

I keep thinking about the people and praying for them every chance I have. I can't imagine going through such a difficult time and not believing in God. There would be no hope.

The Numbers

The World Trade Center

The Twin Towers of the WTC were a place of employment for 50,000 people. City officials are now reporting 4,167 lives lost, while the Red Cross—getting names only from family rather than corporate lists, which could mean duplicates—has the number as low as 2,950. That means that between 91% and 94% of them survived the massacre.

Also, because of the 1993 bombings, changes and upgrades in the safety code had been completed. Fire codes were brought up to snuff; glow paint was laid down in all the stairwells; new alarms were installed along with battery-powered lights. These preparations may be responsible for getting an untold number of lives out of the towers much faster.

The Pentagon

A total of 23,000 people were the target of a third plane aimed at the Pentagon. The latest count shows 123 lost their lives. That is an amazing 99.5% survival rate. In addition, the plane seems to have come in too low, too early to affect a large portion of the building.

On top of that, the section that was hit was the first of five sections to undergo renovation to help protect the Pentagon from terrorist attacks. Being first meant the exact spot of target was prepared in time for the attack. It had recently completed straightening and blast-proofing, saving untold lives.

The Planes

American Airlines Flight 77—This Boeing 757 flown into the Pentagon could have carried up to 289 people, yet only 64 were aboard. Luckily 78% of the seats were empty.

American Airlines Flight 11—This Boeing 767 could have had 351 people aboard, but only carried 92. Thankfully, 74% of the seats were empty.

United Airlines Flight 93—This Boeing 757 was one of the most uplifting stories yet. With the fewest people on board—only 45 people out of a possible 289—it had 84% of its capacity unused. Yet these people stood up to the attackers and thwarted a fourth attempted destruction of a national landmark, saving untold numbers of lives in the process. This was a heroic flight.

United Airlines Flight 175—another Boeing 767 that could have sat 351 people only—had 65 people on board. Fortunately, it was 81% empty.

Out of the 74,280 Americans directly targeted, 95% survived or avoided the attacks. That's a higher survival rate than heart attacks, breast cancer, kidney transplants and liver transplants—all common, survivable illnesses.

The hijacked planes were mostly empty; the Pentagon was hit at its strongest point; the overwhelming majority of people in the World Trade Center buildings escaped; and a handful of passengers gave the ultimate sacrifice to save even more lives.

Listen to your intuition. God works in quiet and mysterious ways.

—Anonymous

Twenty-Nine

"I Am Here"

There will be no more gloom . . . (Isaiah 9:1)

The Scriptures cover all times and all emotions, yet one has to be careful not to take God's Word out of context or bend it to a need, making the Bible appear to say whatever one wants it to say.

But as the e-mails and phone calls and personal conversations began to flow after the attacks, something started to stand out. I began to hear the consistency of the voice within them—it was the same voice I'd heard alone in my own home, the same voice that has spoken throughout the ages. And it seems to be saying, "It's not over yet, but I will still have mercy; rest in Me."

To be very honest, it took me far too long to turn to Scripture. I went to prayer immediately—that's an ever-present conversation—but cracking open the Bible took me longer than it should have.

I live in the center of Manhattan and, though I knew better, I'd opted for the "numb" feeling for the first couple of days. My family was 3,000 miles away and my home was empty. I was within walking distance of so much pain and couldn't find an acceptable place for my own heartache, knowing others nearby were going through so much more.

I knew that the one place you are most in touch with and aware of your emotions is when you're standing face-to-face with the Lord, and in trying to avoid those feelings, I let my fear get the best of me; I shut down. "I'm absolutely fine," I assured myself. "Just give me something to do, and I'll go on from there."

But that's where the Lord found me and wouldn't let me go any further without Him. I called my mother; I called my dearest friend;

I asked for their prayers to figure out where I was most needed at such a time as this—and still, I was neglecting my own prayers.

That is, until my friend said, "That's it—shut everything off and plug in. Don't ask Him in passing where you should be—you're probably not even asking the right question. Sit down, open your Bible and see what He says—not necessarily related to any question you might have. Just see what He says."

Strangely enough, of all the Bibles I've collected over the years, the one I had in my hand at the time wasn't mine. It belonged to the one on the phone giving the advice. It was a gift I had given him at Christmas with his name engraved on the flap: "Stace R. Gaddy." I ran my finger along the engraving, almost afraid to open the flap and let it all in.

The ribbon hadn't been moved since it was purchased and I sat down with my back to my windows and opened to that page to see what on earth the Lord would say.

All right, Lord, I sighed. *Before I bring You my heart, I ask . . . what is on Your heart?* And I began to read. The ribbon fell just to the right of Isaiah 52. Verse two caught my eye first, "Shake yourself from the dust, rise up . . . O captive Daughter of Zion." It went on:

> For thus says the Lord GOD:
> "My people went down at first
>   into Egypt to dwell there;
>   then the Assyrian oppressed them without cause.
> Now therefore, what have I here," says the LORD,
>   "that My people are taken away for nothing?
> Those who rule over them make them wail, . . .
>   and My name is blasphemed continually every day.
> Therefore My people shall know My name;
>   therefore they shall know in that day
>   that I am He who speaks:
> 'Behold, it is I.' " (52:4-6, NKJV)

We have definitely reached a day when, more than I thought I would see in my lifetime, people are asking, "Where is God?" And He is stating in so many ways, "Here I am."

Peggy Noonan, contributing editor for the *Wall Street Journal*, wrote in her article, "Welcome Back, Duke" about two weeks after the attacks:

> For the ignorant, the superstitious and me (and maybe
> you), the face of the Evil One was revealed, and died;
> for the ignorant, the superstitious and me (and maybe
> you), the cross survived. This is how God speaks to us.
> He is saying, "I am," He is saying, "I am here." He is say-
> ing, "And the force of all the evil in the world will not
> bury me."

People were alone in their rooms, offices, studios, gardens, kitchens and cars—wherever they were—asking God, "What's going on?" He was telling them all the same thing—telling us all the same thing. It shouldn't have been a new concept to me. When God's Spirit is so recognizable, and He's the same "yesterday, today and tomorrow," you expect the same voice in different corners of prayer. But it was even more apparent because, now, we are all asking the same question.

> O afflicted city, lashed by storms and not comforted,
> I will build you with stones of turquoise,
>   your foundation with sapphires.
> I will make your battlements of rubies,
>   your gates of sparkling jewels,
>   and all your walls of precious stones.
> All your sons will be taught by the LORD,
>   and great will be your children's peace.
> In righteousness you will be established:
> Tyranny will be far from you;
>   you will have nothing to fear.
> Terror will be far removed;
>   it will not come near you.
> If anyone does attack you, it will not be my doing;
>   whoever attacks you will surrender to you.
>
>   (54:11-15)

And the verses kept coming: attached to e-mails, or the only thing in the e-mail; over the phone; scribbled on corners of suddenly unimportant papers. My father called and read me pieces of Isaiah 9. John Stoos, chief consultant for Senator McClintock, sent out a full two-page e-mail of nothing but straight Scripture. And I must say thank you, by the way, because these verses built me up solidly.

People were comforting one another. Scripture became a gift.

Many of them, in the accompanying stories, mentioned "stumbling" upon their particular verse while looking for a different one, or running into it somehow in the course of their day. Thus the words became messages rather than words we "picked out" to arrange our own comfort.

God, whom we've asked to remove Himself from so many parts of our civilization, is still willing to hold His hand upon us in mercy. He's still willing to answer and to be God, both individually and nationally, if we but call Him to.

It's love. I don't think He could make it much clearer.

Do It Again, Lord

by Max Lucado

We're still hoping we'll wake up. We're still hoping we'll open a sleepy eye and think, "What a horrible dream."

But we won't, will we, Father? What we saw was not a dream. Planes did gouge towers. Flames did consume our fortress. People did perish. It was no dream and, dear Father, we are sad.

There is a ballet dancer who will no longer dance and a doctor who will no longer heal. A church has lost her priest, a classroom is minus a teacher. Cora ran a food pantry. Paige was a counselor and Dana, dearest Father, Dana was only three years old. (Who held her in those final moments?)

We are sad, Father. For as the innocent are buried, our innocence is buried as well. We thought we were safe. Perhaps we should have known better. But we didn't.

And so we come to You. We don't ask You for help; we beg You for it. We don't request it; we implore it. We know what You can do. We've read the accounts. We've pondered the stories and now we plead, "Do it again, Lord. Do it again."

Remember Joseph? You rescued him from the pit. You can do the same for us. Do it again, Lord.

Remember the Hebrews in Egypt? You protected their children from the angel of death. We have children too, Lord. Do it again.

And Sarah? Remember her prayers? You heard them. Joshua? Remember his fears? You inspired him. The women at the tomb? You resurrected their hope. The doubts of Thomas? You took them away. Do it again, Lord. Do it again.

You changed Daniel from a captive into a king's counselor. You took Peter the fisherman and made him Peter, an apostle. Because of You, David went from leading sheep to leading armies. Do it again, Lord, for we need counselors today, Lord. We need apostles. We need leaders. Do it again, dear Lord.

Most of all, do again what you did at Calvary. What we saw here last Tuesday, you saw there that Friday: innocence slaughtered; goodness murdered; mothers weeping; evil dancing. Just as the smoke eclipsed our morning, so the darkness fell on your Son. Just as our towers were shattered, the very Tower of Eternity was pierced.

And by dusk, heaven's sweetest song was silent, buried behind a rock.

But You did not waver, O Lord. You did not waver. After three days in a dark hole, you rolled the rock and rumbled the earth and turned the darkest Friday into the brightest Sunday. Do it again, Lord. Grant us a September Easter.

We thank You, dear Father, for these hours of unity. Christians are praying with Jews. Republicans are standing with Democrats. Skin colors have been covered by the ash of burning buildings. We thank You for these hours of unity.

And we thank You for these hours of prayer. The Enemy sought to bring us to our knees and succeeded. He had no idea, however, that we would kneel before You. And he has no idea what You can do.

Let Your mercy be upon our President, Vice President and their families. Grant to those who lead us wisdom beyond their years and experience. Have mercy upon the souls who have departed and the wounded who remain. Give us grace that we might forgive and faith that we might believe.

And look kindly upon Your Church. For 2,000 years You've used her to heal a hurting world.

Do it again, Lord. Do it again.
Through Christ, Amen.

The Plain Old Power of the Gospel

This book was written, not just for Christians, but for the world—for absolutely everyone. And I pray that whatever you are in need of today—rest, encouragement, hope, healing, a shoulder or His love—I pray that He begins to move again right now and provide for you even the impossible. Whether you've known Him through the ages or are looking for an introduction here, I pray He begins to whisper to your heart that the answer to your need is in the power of the gospel—not just "God," but the gospel.

This book is not about theology; nor do we have the time to go through all the questions, misconceptions, discussions. But I do at least want to address *why* it's not just "God," but the gospel:

Because the gospel is all there is with the true power to change. The gospel can protect us against danger in ways that nothing else can, because He is real.

The word *gospel* means "good news," and that news is this: "God so loved the world that he gave his one and only Son, that whoever believes in him shall not perish but have eternal life" (John 3:16).

Now, whether that's something you believe or not, I want you to know where I am coming from, even if for no other reason than to understand something about your neighbor. When people share the gospel, a common response—one that you may be thinking right now—is, "If you want to believe in Jesus, fine, but why be concerned that others believe the same?"

Why? Because it's like knowing that someone's closest friend—whom they thought didn't exist, or whom, they'd been told, was dead and gone—is not only alive, but is looking for and longing for them. How can I possibly keep it a secret?

I'm not concerned with religion. I don't want to minimize culture or heritage. I simply want you to know that there's Someone who loves you so completely—no matter what—that He died for you. He left all glory behind, and was scorned and broken to get the job done. He walked into the fire.

I could never keep that quiet—not if I cared at all. My only motivation ever for telling His story is absolute love—a love which comes from Him in the first place. It's a love for someone He created, and for the Lord Himself, whose heart's desire is that all would know His love.

His love is not exclusionary, either—it encompasses all peoples, all faiths and beliefs. It is not disrespectful of diversity. It's actually the most inclusive and "politically correct" concept there is: that God loves us and wants us to be one family, with one Father, one thread, one heart. He loves us, regardless of race, creed, sex—and yes, even religion.

He is real, and no matter who you are or where you are right now, I would not have a heart in my body if I didn't take the time, especially in this climate of struggle and restoration, to tell you Jesus loves you. It sounds so elementary. But it is that simple. He just loves you.

For God—the God of Abraham, Isaac and Jacob—so loved the world that He willingly gave His only begotten Son to build a bridge, by his death on the cross, between Himself and the human race, which is separated so far from Him by sin. He did this so that there might be an everlasting reunion—so that whoever believes in Him will not perish, but have eternal life. He bars no one from heaven; the doors to glory, as well as His heart, His arms and His life, are wide open. We only turn ourselves away.

He is a jealous God—jealously protective of His children. He fights for them to take His hand because He knows He holds the only authoritative power over evil and death. He doesn't want these things to touch His children.

So when Jesus says, "I am the way and the truth and the life. No one comes to the Father except through me" (14:6), He is not slamming a door or insisting that we worship Him. It's more like the plea of a rescue worker who says, "Take my hand. I am the only one up here and I've been through the fire, so I know there is no other way out. But I've made a way for you. Trust me. Come with me."

If He wanted to, He could override our free will and *make* us call Him God. But He gave us a choice so it could be called love.

I would be remiss if I did not invite you to meet Him now, if you haven't already. He's been there all the time; He is with you now. There is no ceremony to it. The plainest language is a song to His ears. Don't take my word for it, or anyone else's; ask Him yourself.

You can say the prayer that follows if you are at a loss for words. But it's between you and God to talk and there are no wrong words. Though it only takes one decision, and a heart that means it, to change a life entirely and eternally, it's still my own prayer with each new day:

> *Jesus, come into my life. Forgive me the sins that I fall to repeatedly, the lazy things I let pull me away from seeing the world through Your eyes and the large things that tear apart the beauty that You would have for my life and others. Remove by Your name all the things that separate me from You. I acknowledge it as sin. And I would rather have Your way. I believe in You. I trust in You. I see what You have done. Show me more of You and who You are.*
>
> *Be God in this world. Be Lord of my life. This, for all people. And by Your grace, grant me Jesus.*

So why not just "God," but the gospel? Because the gospel is the enabler in the equation. The gospel lasts. His Holy Spirit is where the power is to endure and to overcome. His Holy Spirit is what lifts the darkness and breaks apart despair, to bring real joy in all circumstances.

We heard from heroes like Lisa Beamer, who stepped up to the plate to tell not only how God can do these things, but that He also has already, for her and so many others. When times become extreme, miracles can follow. If we put Him at the helm, acknowledge God and hand Him back the world that is His, it would not be unimaginable for a hijacked plane to disappear into thin air when we call on the name of the One who can do all things. There would be real healing. There would be lasting peace. And there could be.

In a recent interview, Anne Graham Lotz, daughter of Billy Graham stated:

> We've asked [God] to get out of our lives and out of our country. It's OK if He stays in the churches and synagogues. But leave everything else alone.
>
> He could have done exactly as we asked. Some say He already did. I'd say He's holding out His mercy; that on September 11th He wept and offered this chance: "Tell Me to stay, tell Me not to let go of you. I will not force My love on you. But I am here. Tell Me to stay."

Join me in asking Him to stay. Ask Him with our prayers, the way we live our lives, every decision that we make—even the ones that seem small and insignificant. Make even those decisions according to His way, and watch what He will do with that faith! Ask Him with our votes, with how we treat one another, how we run our homes and schools, how we love our families and strangers. Ask Him together, and tell His story boldly. Our own story, then, will be authored by His hands, and it will be written perfectly.

> *Dear Lord, be Lord. Be Lord of my life. Be Lord of our country. Forgive us our embarrassing audacity in trying to take the character of the world away from its Creator. And forgive us too, for forgetting how You've held our land, blessed us beyond measure with peace, safety, freedom. We are not blind to the ills that have been performed in the name of America. But at our foundation, Father, at our core, we hope to be the light on the hill, to help and to heal, to be a land of brothers and an example of that solidarity to the world. We cannot do this without Your healing hand.*
>
> *It's so simple: God, we need You.*
>
> *We don't call to You because we want to be "prosperous and untouchable," the highest power in the world. We call to You because You are God and because, at our base, we*

want to love one another. We long for peace—between all people. We long for Jesus.

There is no greater love.

A Call to Arms, a Prayer, a Farewell . . .

America, it's time to get started—not time to put our past behind us, but time to put our past before us. Remember it always. Remember the mistakes and the victories. Remember to be grateful. Remember that Providence has always held us fast—even in our shortcomings. God in His mercy has caught us every time and He's holding us now.

"If my people, who are called by my name, will humble themselves and pray and seek my face and turn from their wicked ways, then will I hear from heaven and will forgive their sin and will heal their land" (2 Chronicles 7:14).

> *Forgive us, Lord, that we have not seen You entirely for what You are. Forgive us that we have not realized Your love. Show us anew, Lord, in a world where the message has been distorted and adulterated, where people have been lied to even in Your name, where we have forgotten our first love, show us anew. Open our eyes, ears and hearts afresh to the light that is Yours. Only Your Spirit can make it clear. Talk to us, Lord, individually and as a nation. Talk loudly and don't let go. Restore us together, but even more wonderfully show us Your love personally . . . each one. For all those who don't know You, speak to their hearts that they may know how much You love them—let there be a great reunion, Lord, as all Your children recognize You.*
>
> *Give us unconditional love for one another. Let nothing stand in our way; let nothing translate into personal judgment. Let us see all people as the family that we are.*
>
> *And thank You, Lord. Thank You for a chance to try again, to get better at this living and at the way we're acting toward each other. Thank You for Your unwavering love. Thank You that Your heart is full for our sake.*

Thank You that there is a land yet under Your mercy, a place to hope and rebuild. Thank You that there was not greater destruction within our boundaries. Thank You for our leaders who gathered in the rotunda of the Capitol to seek Your blessings and, amazingly, to find them. Continue to call them.

Thank You for America. We are trying, Lord, to be the light on the hill. We are trying.

Go before us, God, to all the world. Set the hearts of all the nations at peace with one another. Be our fortress; for we know that there is evil in this world, but that You hold all authority over the powers of evil if we would only invite you to be Lord of this world. We could be in Your hands if we only accepted Your free invitation. Guide us to trust You. Sometimes it's so hard to see Your plan of redemption when so much has changed. Remind us effectively that You have not changed, and that You never will. Take us, Lord, take us forward.

Respecting my brothers and sisters of all faiths, I pray passionately in Jesus' name, Amen.

Don't ever let the prayer end.

Afterword

I want you to know what God has done to bring this book to you—the battles and miracles that transpired, and the evidences that came to show God knows tomorrow. Because if you've been reading this, it's what He's done for you. There is something here that He wants you to have: comfort, rest, understanding, strength—maybe even His eternal life.

I want you to know what God has done to bring this book to you.

In order to share that, and to fully tell the story of September 11, 2001, I have to go back almost a decade. God was moving the pieces even then to prepare us—preparing our hearts, preparing the world, preparing to be our comfort. This story is a minute part of what I know God was doing around the world as we headed unknowingly toward this tragedy. But it's one example of how He begins to keep our steps before we even ask, before we make the decision to be faithful, before we meet the point of need.

Before we even exist, He is making a way.

Ten years ago I came to New York, not necessarily of my own desire, but because of circumstances I felt sure the Lord had intended. So I left my family on the West Coast and came to meet Manhattan—not knowing why, unable to imagine a far-off September when the inconceivable would unfold.

Manhattan wasn't easy for a northern California native who was very aware of the importance of family. I spent most of my time in prayer trying to figure out when I'd be able to go back home. I survived four years at New York University, vowing I would leave the day after gradu-

201

ation. I mean no disrespect to the city with the incomparable character—the city watched over me in my time of greatest trial. It challenged me and asked me all the tough questions I'd never been asked before. But I was answering many of them incorrectly and I wanted out.

The shock of learning just how wrong I could be brought me face-to-face with a God I thought I knew. Every attempt I made to leave was met with a directive to stay. I still fought, as we human beings tend to do when God is most at work; it's often when we become our most stubborn.

Upon graduation, I was given an offer I couldn't refuse, one that would require my staying on the East Coast. It arrived as an application in my mailbox marked, "Enclosed is the information you requested." I had never requested it—neither had any of the friends and family I interrogated on the subject. So I stayed.

It came to be a constant procedure in my life: the insistence on leaving, the Hand that encouraged the staying. He never forced me, never made it impossible to leave—He just made it clear that I shouldn't and gave me the opportunity to obey.

I wasn't the best at it. I complained when I should have been grateful; I cried when I was really so blessed. In one particular moment of those tears, someone—who knew nothing of why my tears were being shed—said to me in the lobby of a church, "The biggest mistake people sometimes make is giving up just before the task is at hand."

This spiritual, geographic tug-of-war continued, never varying from the nature of its influence: "Stay in New York. There is a reason. There is work to be done." *Yes, Lord. No matter what.*

A few years ago, there came a particularly unexpected twist in this New York experience. Still weighing the options of leaving, I was offered a position as Editor in *Guideposts'* Books and Media Division. This was even more peculiar considering I had not applied for the job and I was not seeking full-time employment. I wasn't even fully qualified for the position at the time. I could do the job, but I didn't have the experience behind me that would convince those who hired me that I deserved the job. And yet they gave it to me—unexpectedly, immediately.

I started on the second day of March. That morning I climbed in a cab to avoid the subways—I didn't want to risk a train delay and be late on the first day.

As a freelancer and performer in New York City, I'd never had a full-time job, never had a mandatory, everyday, 9 a.m. call to go to an office, with a desk and two chairs that would be mine. It would be a foreign world to me; even the commute was unfamiliar.

I smiled at the entertaining unpredictability of life in God's hands, and caught my image in the cab window, played against the moving reflections of the buildings on Broadway. I sat with my hands in my lap and wondered where on earth the Lord was taking me now. I couldn't have known then, but it was not lost on me. Whatever it was, I felt it.

I had an electronic Bible in my purse, given to me by a very dear family. It had a "verse of the day" program, so I turned it on to see what Word might be prepared for such a day as this. It was Revelation 21:4-5, and it was astoundingly perfect:

> And God will wipe away every tear from their eyes; there shall be no more death, nor sorrow, nor crying. There shall be no more pain, for the former things have passed away.
>
> Then He who sat on the throne said, "Behold, I make all things new." And He said to me, "*Write*, for these words are true and faithful" (emphasis added, NKJV).

It was poignant enough at the time. I wiped away a tear, born from remembering how precisely God plans our every step—and that, according to His purpose. I wrote it in a notebook, knowing there was probably more purpose in it than I could see then, and I resolved to watch for it.

But again, I could have never imagined then, as my cab traveled down Broadway through an empty, early-morning Times Square—oddly enough, at about 8:45, on my way to a 9 o'clock job—what I would experience from the same streets at the same hour on September 11, 2001.

And Again He Said, "Write!"

Two months before the attack, I felt prompted to join a local Bible study. It would be only the second time I'd done so in my nine-and-a-half years in the city (Bible studies are a little tougher under city circumstances; the transportation alone made one think twice about making a long-term, weekly commitment.) But this was one of those nudgings I couldn't ignore.

On the very first meeting I shared all the details of my testimony including the struggle to stay, the concern over spending so many years away from loved ones, and the certainty that, despite it all, there was a reason.

We began studying Henry Blackaby's book, *Being God's Friend*, and by the time we covered the second unit—"God's Fullness of Time"—I was faced with a couple of tough questions that God seemed to be bringing to my attention. I scribbled a note in the margin of the workbook that read,

> Am I willing to write even if that means closing the door on music? Yes, Lord—incontestably, yes. Though I ask for the opportunity of both, if the question is, "Would I do one if it meant giving up the other," then You have my commitment. Just let me know clearly [note choice of word] which is Your will and that is what I shall do. Regardless of path or capacity, here am I.

If you knew me, you would know the magnitude of my penning such a thought. Music has always been my most directing passion and my number-one career focus; writing came second. I had avoided God's nudges to write, under the excuse that I didn't know where to start or what to do.

That wasn't the only note, either. I also wrote at the bottom of that page, "I've begun to realize I may have been deaf to the writing assignment bullhorns. Show me anew, Lord. What, when and where . . . I have fresh ears. I'll do it."

A portion of the text on that page read, "Only in immediate obedience would we later see the serious implications of that moment in time for us." Sensing God was saying more than I'd yet understood, I continued to comment in the margins, "Regarding the writing assignments, I've picked up the inklings but wonder if it's not a more dire call and command. I think there's something waiting to be heard."

This all would have been substantiation enough in itself, but then, five pages later, Blackaby shared his own adjustment-of-direction story—and the words with which he chose to tell it seemed a reprint of my marginal notes in the previous unit.

"I faced such a moment in my own life," he began. He describes how he had the question posed to him, "What has God been wanting you to do that you've not yet done?" His single thought was, "Writing." He prayed, "O Lord, my Lord, if You clearly [note choice of word], unmistakably, undeniably are showing me that I should write, I promise I will respond immediately."

When a colleague approached him with a writing suggestion, he responded, "Do you clearly [note choice of word], unmistakably, undeniably feel I should write this?" He went on to tell this colleague, "Only yesterday did I make a solemn commitment to write if God should clearly [note choice of word] show me that I should." I read this the day after I had made an identical commitment.

There is much more, but Blackaby ends the page saying, "God will be honored and many people will be greatly blessed. . . ." Unbelievably, I wrote beneath that, "This is a promise, I feel it. Something starts right here, if it's Your time Lord."

More than ever in this world, now is the time when people are bending their ear, their soul, to the spirit of the Lord. If it is His time, and how greatly it seems that it is, then I pray that "God will be honored and many people will be greatly blessed. . . ."

This was August. I could never have guessed what would transpire in the coming month. I didn't know what to do to respond to the "only in immediate obedience" suggestion. So I bought a laptop and I waited.

A Charge to Keep

In the days following September 11th, I spent uncounted hours on the phone with my parents. "Everything is fleeting" was the new awareness, and people latched on to those they love. We talked endlessly just to "be" with each other, despite the miles between us, to calm each other's worries and to carry each other through.

In one such conversation, my father and I talked for an hour about nothing before he finally got around to what he'd been trying to say. Actually in tears—an uncommon thing for him—he said, "God is going to use you."

The way he said it was unusual. I know my father's voice; he was not saying this phrase with an everyday, "you are where you are for a reason" tone of simple encouragement. This was a sense that God had a specific work to be done, an urgent feeling. On the edge of my seat I said to my father, and to my heavenly Father concurrently, "OK. Yes."

Hardly a profound response, but there was nothing else I could say or was supposed to say. I was meant simply to know and, when I had the chance, to obey—whatever it would be.

My mother also gave me a charge the same day: she told me to write. Naming other historical turns our country has faced in the last half century, she emphasized the responsibility of *communication* and *remembrance*. (It is not surprising that my mother should stress these two things; she works for KFIA/KTKZ Radio in Sacramento, and is an author as well. She also served in Taiwan during the Vietnam War.)

She underscored the importance of being here in New York at "such a time as this." And she told me to write it down. I didn't know where to begin, but I knew her charge and my father's statement were both a tap on the shoulder from the Lord.

I watched and I waited. I wrote a few articles for the KTKZ web site. In my human way of underestimating what God has planned and what He wants to do for people, I thought that was it. I had written, right? I had written of Him and sent it out to the world through a northern California radio station web site. Sure, with God there's always more, but I thought it would come over the course of the rest of my lifetime as I shared His love with the inhabitants of a changed world, from the point of view of someone who was in this city when it began. That may still be true, and I'm sure it is for all of us, no matter where we were when these events commenced. But that day, I got a call from someone I barely knew. I was asked, by title, to complete this manuscript, *Be Still, America*. I didn't have to take the time to think about it. It was clear.

Though I began work that same day, it was a couple of weeks until I remembered the verse that had appeared years before, on the day my focus shifted to ministry through the written word. This meant so much more than mere affirmation that this task would be God's work and the results His as well. So much more than that, it meant that He *knew*.

He knew what would happen and He began even then, so long before, to provide.

You can take this to heart for all circumstances, not just for the current trying times. Good or bad, large or small, individual or global, He knows. He has known since before time began what we would face, what choices we would make, what we would need and feel. In His provision is the promise that He will always provide, for His character does not change. He is "the same yesterday and today and forever" (Hebrews 13:8).

Under the new circumstances in the world, I now understand the work that He was doing beforehand, and all my prior complaining and whining about the details of endurance becomes so small when studied under the glass of God's heart for His people. Wherever you are, don't judge your work or circumstances by the measure of yourself or your feelings. Judge them by Him and by the need of others. It's suddenly so much more worth anything it takes.

In that same spirit, this book is not for me. The above message about the movements of His hands in my life is not about bringing this book to pass for *me*. If you are reading this, He did it for *you*. His story is in here, how He heals, loves, prepares, restores. The gospel is in here in action. It's not just the basics; it's how the gospel unfolds in people's lives.

My prayer is that any question or fear or weight you carry in your heart will be carried instead by the Lord—whatever it is you're dealing with in the wake of September 11 or decades from now. He speaks to us individually. I pray you will seek and find all that He wants to give to you.

Back when I first found that now-weighted verse, I laughed at what I thought was the tongue-in-cheek message from Lord in the first half of it—that there would be "no more crying" over the transitional stages of my life (at the time, typical post-college frustrations like temp jobs and missing family). But when I revisited the verse after beginning this book, the full scope of His message unfurled. He was speaking already of the tears that September 11th would set to raining—and of the sorrow, pain and death we would face, saying He will make all things new.

I wish I knew His voice well enough to have understood years ago. It's a strange feeling to realize only now what He was saying then—and that He knew. It's a heavy thing on the heart to know His heart was hurting, knowing the tragedy we were about to endure. But in His care, He was preparing our comfort, and He began with His Word. In this new, post-September 11 world, I read the verse again.

> "And God will wipe away every tear from their eyes; there shall be no more death, nor sorrow, nor crying. There shall be no more pain, for the former things have passed away." Then He who sat on the throne said, "Behold, I make all things new." And then He said to me, "Write, for these words are true and faithful." (Revelation 21:4-5, NKJV)

In one way or another, He will "wipe every tear" from our eyes, and He will "make all things new." So I follow His lead, the history He designed and guided, and I "write" what I hope is His message to you. If I have delivered His message without getting too much in the way, then indeed "these words are true and faithful." I leave you with the stories of what the Lord has done.

It is my hope that within them you've heard His heart and voice saying, "Be still. I am here. I am God. You are before My eyes at all times. And I love you. Be still in your heart and listen to My ways, My Words. They are spoken because I care for you."

I have seen Him, through all those I've met through this book—I have heard Him in their conversations and in my own time alone with God as I remembered them. I have seen His light in their eyes, no matter what they've seen in the course of their day. Men who spent their day encountering gruesome sights, smiled; with tears in their eyes, they smiled. You could see the Lord holding them—it simply radiated. People who lost husbands, wives or children spoke peacefully, gratefully of God's care as they began to go on. People can't stop working to help others; they can't keep from telling what God has done for them in all of this—even people who have lost so much.

His voice is ringing loudly, His face everywhere I turn. He is telling His story in one way or another through people's lives and by His Spirit. May we hear Him. May we see Him. May we respond to the calling of His heart when He calls us by name. And may we never forget the good or the bad—the lessons or the testimony; the history. God is on His throne, and He's already told us how this story ends.

Be still, America. Be still, all nations of people. Be still and *know* that He is God.

If you are interested in having the author speak at your church or event, or for more information, please contact:

Amy Bartlett Ministries
info@amybartlett.com
or visit
www.amybartlett.com

A portion of the proceeds of this book will go to the Todd M. Beamer Memorial Foundation, Inc. Further contributions are being received on the web site www.beamerfoundation.org, or at the following mailing address:

Todd M. Beamer Memorial Foundation, Inc.
P.O. Box 32
Cranbury, NJ 08512